BLOSSOMS
IN THE
DESERT

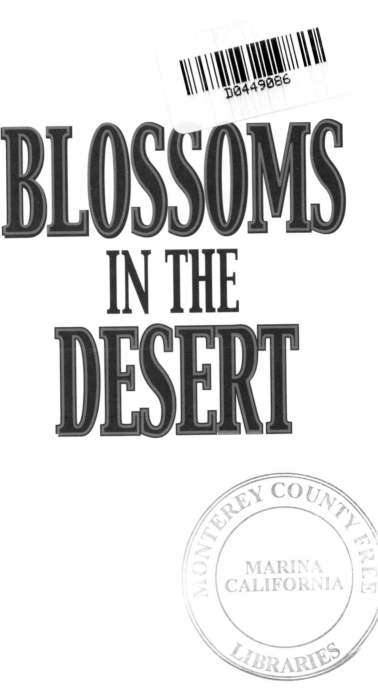

Edited by Darrell Y. Hamamoto

Produced by Topaz High School Class of 1945.

For orders and information, contact:
P.O. Box 31397, San Francisco, CA 94131-0397 **or**
109 Gladeview Way – San Francisco, CA 94131-1214

Major funding for this book provided by the California Civil Liberties Public Education Program.

Cover – Woodblock Print of Topaz High School: © 1970 Miye Yoshimori Yoshida

All written material is previously unpublished.

   Blossoms in the Desert – Topaz High School Class of 1945, edited by
      Darrell Y. Hamamoto
      Produced by Topaz High School Class of 1945
      Includes bibliographical references
      1. Japanese Americans – Evacuation and relocation, 1942-1945.
      2. World War II, 1941-1945 – Japanese Americans – personal interviews.
         Members of Topaz High School Class of 1945
      3. Concentration camps – United States – History – 20th century.
         I. Hamamoto, Darrell Y.
         II. Topaz High School Class of 1945

Blossoms in the Desert: Topaz High School Class of 1945 /
Darrell Y. Hamamoto (editor)

ISBN 0-9744653-0-5

Printing by Giant Horse Printing, Inc., South San Francisco, California, USA.
www.gianthorse.com

DEDICATION

To the memory of our parents,
Issei pioneers who struggled mightily against
the forces of racial discrimination.
And to those classmates who are no longer
with us to share the rich experiences of
fellow Topaz High School students who
came of age in a U.S. concentration camp.

CONTENTS

PREFACE

Blossoms In The Desert – Topaz High Class of 1945 – Our Story in an American Concentration Camp, is the collective effort of members of the Topaz High School Class of 1945, which recounts the experiences of their growing up and receiving their entire high school education from September 1942–June 1945, within the confines of the Topaz Concentration Camp in Utah.

Of the 8,000 plus persons imprisoned in Topaz, the high school class of 1945 numbered some 254. This class included those who graduated in January 1945, June 1945, as well as the January 1946 class members who had enough course credits to graduate with the June class before the camp closed.

Their average age was about 14 years old at the time when they and their families were uprooted from their homes and imprisoned in a hastily-built compound in a harsh, remote desert. The student body came from various urban and rural settings, from San Francisco's Japantown to remote farms located in Washington. No matter what their background, they found their three years in camp to be perhaps the most impressionable years of their lives. From a sociological and psychological point of view, they were forced to cope with circumstances that few teenagers had to face. Adjustment to loss, dislocation and uncertainty, was compounded by having to live in a confined environment where personal privacy was non-existent.

The idea for this book was born in Washington, D.C., in November of 2000, during the dedication of the National Japanese American Memorial to Patriotism during World War II. The Topaz Class of 1945 gathered for a class dinner in conjunction with this historic event. Several classmates talked informally of their internment experience and the stories were parallel and yet so diverse.

After realizing the impact these differences had on their existence and future development, the group raised the possibility of preserving these precious memories. The stories could describe in some measure the hopes, the joys, the outrage, the camaraderie, the deepest fears for the future of their families, and their loyalty to the country of their birth which had been so severely questioned. Yet the years at Topaz High provided an identity that the former students are proud of, forming bonds of unity, a sense of closeness, and of deep friendship. These bonds have resulted in twenty-three reunions of this class since their first get-together in 1970 in commemoration of their 25th year reunion.

The idea did not fade away after that dinner. Taking the lead in pursuing and creating a collection of classmates' experiences were Glenn "Rosie" Kumekawa of Rhode Island, and Paul Bell, a Caucasian and son of Roscoe Bell, deputy director of the Topaz camp, of Pennsylvania, took the lead. They conferred with Daisy Satoda (nee Uyeda) of San Francisco and several other classmates. Daisy explored some possibilities, and was encouraged by Diane Matsuda, director of the California Civil Liberties Education Program, (CCLPEP) to develop and conserve these unique experiences and remembrances. By December of that year, a core group that included Ron "Tubby Yoshida" of Northridge, CA, and George "Dorsey" Kobayashi of St. Louis, MO, discussed applying for a grant from CCLPEP to fund the publication of a book.

After the group met several times in 2001, they developed a strategic framework to achieve their goal. Later that year they asked Darrell Hamamoto, PhD, Asian American Studies professor at the University of California Davis, to serve as editor of the book. Kenzo Ishimaru of San Jose, CA, and Kumi Ishida of San Mateo, CA were added to the committee, and later Kenzo agreed to serve as project co-ordinator.

The group's application to the CCLPEP resulted in the successful award of a grant in May of 2002, to write the book about the Topaz High Class of 1945.

A questionnaire was sent to class members to enlist their participation and generate information. Classmates were asked to describe their lives as students in a school with little educational materials and a makeshift school campus providing minimal contact with the outside world and the impact this had on their education, social, and cultural experiences. Many student left camp shortly after graduation, and others, when only 16 and 17 years old, left on their own for the Midwest and East to complete their education in unknown and oftentimes hostile communities and situations.

Questionnaires were analyzed, oral history interviews were conducted, and some classmates wrote their own personal histories. The interviews recalled the impact of those three years of confinement, not only on education, but on the toll that was exacted in the breakdown of the traditional family unit. Lives were governed by a peer society where students spent much of their time together because most of their social interactions took place at school and the activities therein. There was nowhere else to go to form other relationships or to pursue outside interests. Because most families lived in single rooms with no extra space to entertain guests, friends could not visit each other in the barracks.

The interviews also brought out the strength of the friendships that were formed during those high school years. Since there was no exposure to social or cultural contacts with outside communities or schools, except for athletes competing against nearby high schools, all interactions among the students were restricted to the mono-ethnic student body at Topaz High.

The book remembers those who have preceded the contributors and also reflects on the events that occurred sixty years ago by rediscovering the bonds of common experience of the members of the class within the confines of barbed wire fences, guarded by armed sentries, in a concentration camp named Topaz, which has been returned to the desert from which it arose.

These stories of incarceration and education in a concentration camp during World War II, unique in the annals of our country's history, are our collective legacy to succeeding generations to ensure that such a travesty of justice never again befalls any other group of people in this country.

* * * *

Paul "Shorty" Bell, State College, PA
Kumi Ishida, San Mateo, CA
Kenzo Ishimaru, San Jose, CA, project coordinator
George "Dorsey" Kobayashi, St. Louis, MO
Glenn "Rosie" Kumekawa, Wakefield, RI
Daisy Uyeda Satoda. San Francisco, CA
Ron "Tubby" Yoshida, Northridge, CA

September, 2003.

ACKNOWLEDGMENTS

The Book Committee of the Topaz, Utah, High School Class of 1945 would like to thank:

- The participating class members who shared the bittersweet memories of their personal wartime experience of completing their entire high school education from 1942-1945, while imprisoned behind barbed wire. The oral history interviews were conducted under the leadership of Kenzo Ishimaru, Kumi Ishida, and Daisy Uyeda Satoda. Other interviewers and questionnaire organizers were book committee members: Paul Bell, George "Dorsey" Kobayashi, and Ron "Tubby" Yoshida. Also assisting in this phase of our project were: Darrell Hamamoto, Sachi Kawahara Masaoka, Diane Matsuda, and Somao Ochi.

- The California Civil Liberties Public Education Program (CCLPEP) and members of its Advisory Board for the funding received to publish this book. Dr. Kevin Starr, State Librarian, and the staff of the California State Library, which administers the CCLPEP program.

- To give public recognition to Diane Matsuda, Program Director of CCLPEP, for her encouragement to write our story and the invaluable assistance she has given throughout this project.

- We are indebted to then Assembly member Mike Honda, and now Congressperson from San Jose, who introduced the California Civil Liberties Public Education Act in the California State Assembly in 1998. The original three-year program was extended an additional two years through legislation introduced by Assembly member George Nakano of Torrance.

- The Japanese Cultural and Community Center of Northern California (JCCCNC), under the direction of Executive Director Paul Osaki, for providing us with meeting rooms for the past two years and the continuing support by staff members Jill Shiraki, Sandy Kajiyama, Jennifer Hamamoto, Ruby Hata, Mike Furutani, and others.

- Giant Horse Printing, Inc., in South San Francisco, for producing this book with artistic and printing expertise provided by Jeannie Yee, publisher.

- Members of Topaz High Class of 1945 for their financial contributions which provided the "seed money" to embark on this project.

- Editor Darrell Hamamoto, PhD, professor of Asian American Studies, University of California at Davis, who distilled our oral history interviews and developed them into this book, *Blossoms in the Desert – Topaz High School Class of 1945*.

Acknowledgment and thanks for the generous loan of photographs, painting, and other memorabilia:

- Miye Yoshida for the woodblock print from Topaz High Class of 1945's 25th year reunion dinner, 1970, which is used on the front cover.

- Drawings and paintings by Siberius Saito, courtesy of Ruth Saito of San Mateo.

- Chiura Obata drawings/paintings provided by Kimi Kodani Hill of Berkeley

- Photos of Topaz by Kameo Kido and Yas Furuya. Other photos provided by Bob Utsumi, Daisy Satoda, Yayoe Matsuura, The Ramblings yearbook, Kumi Ishida, and others.

- A GI mackinaw provided by Yoneo Kawakita of San Mateo.

- Drawing of Topaz High Library by Ella Honderich, courtesy of Japanese American National Museum.

- Sketches of Tanforan and Topaz by Mike Mickey Suzuki, courtesy of Nami Suzuki.

- Topaz Dance Bids provided by Kazuko Hashiguichi Iwasaki.

INTRODUCTION

World events conspired to disrupt and fundamentally alter the course of Japanese American life after a remote US Naval installation called Pearl Harbor was decimated in a preemptive military strike by the forces of Imperial Japan on December 7, 1941. Years of popular anti-Japanese American hostility fomented by labor unions, nativist organizations, demagogues, and politicians culminated in the issuance of Executive Order 9066 by President Franklin D. Roosevelt on February 19, 1942. This led to the forcible removal and relocation of approximately 120,000 persons of Japanese descent—the majority of them US citizens—to ten different concentration camps hastily erected in desolate areas in the western part of the country.

Blossoms In the Desert is a collection of thoughts and memories by a unique group of former internees who were united by shared experiences as students enrolled in the last graduating class of Topaz High School—the "Class of '45." As sons and daughters of *Issei* immigrants who had formed communities throughout Northern California, they were uprooted and taken first to Tanforan race track in San Bruno, California and then sent to their final destination at the Topaz concentration camp (officially designated as "Central Utah WRA Relocation Center") located in Millard County, sixteen miles northwest of Delta, Utah. At

Tanforan, makeshift classes were taught by fellow Japanese American internees and held outdoors in The Grandstand. Once resettled at Topaz, White teachers joined their unfree Japanese American counterparts to staff the faculty of the high school.

The students and teachers at Topaz High tried to recreate the features of typical American school life on the outside. Involvement with academics, athletics, student government, service organizations, and social events played an important role in the everyday life of the average Topaz High schooler. Outside the classroom, the students of Topaz High School also learned about themselves as young people verging on adulthood. Tentative first steps were taken in romance, adventure, and vocation through their participation in school dances, teenage pranks, and camp work assignments. For most, their experience as students at Topaz High School remained the touchstone of their extraordinary lives.

Many of those interviewed for this collection spoke with deep respect and affection for the more gifted teachers. Some respondents were equally as quick to identify those teachers who obviously lacked in qualifications and commitment to the social and intellectual development of their students. Despite the substandard conditions in which teachers and students were forced to work, it is remarkable that so many in the Class of '45 went on to earn university degrees and achieved personal and professional distinction later in life. This stands in tribute to the dedicated teachers—some of them Japanese American internees like the often-mentioned Dave Tatsuno, Rose Watanabe, and Eiko Hosoi—and parents who viewed education as their best opportunity for achieving substantive equality in a hostile society.

The *Nisei* teenage world they had fashioned out of 1940s American popular culture included the music of the Big Bands, Hollywood movie stars, sports heroes, and radio personalities. Whether from the city or the country—a defining distinction among internees—youngsters at Topaz were immersed in the larger currents of contemporary American culture and society. In camp, they fashioned a distinctive Japanese American youth culture that paralleled that of the world outside the guarded gates. Expressions of that culture included involvement with baseball leagues, the Boy Scouts, dance bands, jitterbug dance contests, and keeping abreast of fashions that might include zoot suits, peplum dresses, or ducktail hairdos. Unlike their high school contemporaries who lived in freedom, however, Japanese American youth culture was created and practiced under conditions of mass racial imprisonment. The superficial normalcy of Topaz High—with its newspaper (*Ram-Bler*) and yearbook (*Ramblings*), student council, homecoming dances, assemblies, movie nights, athletic contests, and a graduation ceremony complete with cap and gown—seemed both to embrace and mock the conventions of high school life beyond the guard towers.

The destabilization of the family structure under conditions of camp life is a theme often repeated among *Nisei* former internees. Although the erosion of *Issei* authority resulted in greater individual autonomy for their children, as adults many *Nisei* came to understand that this marginal gain in personal "freedom" was achieved only at great cost to their parents. Many of those represented in these pages express wonder at the unspeakable hardships endured by their parents in being forcibly removed from their homes and losing almost every material possession in the process. The family was further fragmented in cases where relatives were held in distant concentration camps. Others were released to attend school outside the mandated security zone. Some were given the dubious option of enlisting in the US military while their imprisoned parents awaited an uncertain fate in camp.

Topaz Relocation Center officially closed on October 31, 1945. At its peak, approximately 8,130 people lived within its confines. Prior to its closing, select internees had managed to escape Topaz by leaving for military service, finding outside jobs, and attending schools in the Midwest and East. Most, however, were faced with the challenge of return and resettlement upon their release. Despite assistance from family friends, community and church organizations, and government, the return and resettlement of former internees was difficult at best. Many found that hostility toward Japanese Americans had not abated after the war as they attempted to rebuild lives that had been profoundly disrupted by the internment. One of the contributors to this anthology spoke of riding on a train shortly after the war ended and being taunted by a uniformed GI who called out to him as if he were a dog. Less obvious were the internalized, hidden injuries of internment that became manifest over the years that followed.

After being released from camp, the graduates of Topaz High School Class of '45 sought a sense of normalcy like most Americans in the postwar years. They found jobs, pursued educational opportunities, married and raised families, and built careers. But because they were thrust together under horrible circumstances at a singular moment in their young lives, the Class of '45 exhibited a high degree of social cohesion that remains to this day. As they settled into their middle years, key class members began organizing yearly reunions where they could relive the good times and the bad. The first reunion was held on August 1, 1970 at the Miyako Hotel in *Nihonmachi* or "Japantown" section of San Francisco.

According to principal organizers of the 1970 inaugural class reunion, the gathering was intended to be purely social in nature. There was no political agenda that underlay their desire to reunite twenty-five years after being released from Topaz. But even as former internees began making sense of their camp experiences on a personal level, a parallel movement was afoot to bring to public attention the grave injustice done by the US government in its mass imprisonment of Japanese Americans during the war. The seeds of the redress and reparations movement were sown in the decade of the 1970s, culminating in the Civil Rights Act of 1988 that acknowledged the "fundamental injustice of the evacuation, relocation, and internment of United States citizens and permanent resident aliens of Japanese ancestry during World War II." An official apology by the US government and restitution to those interned were among the provisions of Public Law 100-383 enacted by Congress.

One of the stated reasons for the 1988 Civil Rights Act was to "discourage the occurrence of similar injustices and violations of civil liberties in the future." As a consequence, a trust fund was established within the Treasury Department called the "Civil Liberties Public

Education Fund." At the state level, the California Civil Liberties Public Education Program (CCLPEP) was established to fund projects designed to heighten awareness of the internment and its far-reaching implications for all Americans. *Blossoms in the Desert* is one of many historically important community projects that were realized through funds provided through the CCLPEP as administered by the California State Public Library headed by Dr. Kevin Starr.

In sharing stories at the Topaz High School reunions, classmates came to understand that their camp experiences had profound meaning beyond that of their close circle of friends. They began imagining the possibility of interviewing high school classmates to tell the story of their internment from a perspective only partially captured in historical accounts, sociological studies, and literary work. In conversations with Diane Matsuda, CCLPEP Program Director, they learned that there were relatively few projects devoted to the Topaz Relocation Center. She encouraged them to submit a proposal for an oral history project that would convey the lived-experience of their high school class. Several drafts later, the principal organizers of the oral history research project submitted the proposal that resulted in the present collection of highly personal stories, *Blossoms in the Desert.*

Stories such as those found in this volume are of even greater importance in post-9/11 America. The subterranean river of racism that feeds a society founded upon mass removal, genocide, slavery, incarceration, territorial annexation, and colonialism once more broke forcefully to the surface after the preeminent symbols of US militarism and capitalism—The Pentagon and The World Trade

Center—were attacked by agents of those countries committed to resisting the imperial designs of the last remaining superpower. Vicious physical assaults and incendiary rhetoric directed against Arab Americans, Muslims, and Asian Americans who supposedly "looked" like Arabs followed in immediate response to the concerted attack upon the US "homeland."

On February 4, 2003 US Representative Howard Coble (R-North Carolina) appeared on a radio program in Greensboro, North Carolina, and spoke with a caller who argued that Arab Americans should be sent to internment camps in keeping with the so-called war on terrorism. While he did not necessarily agree with the caller, Coble did concede that "some of these Arab Americans are probably intent on doing harm to us today." In making his point, the congressman invoked the example of the internment of Japanese Americans during World War II and justified the government's decision to do so. Coble stated that not only did some Japanese Americans pose a threat during wartime, but they needed protection from potential harm because "it wasn't safe for them to be on the street."

In immediate response to the controversy inspired by Rep. Coble, a coalition of Asian American civil rights organization called for his resignation as Chair of the House Judiciary Subcommittee on Crime, Terrorism and Homeland Security. Fellow members of Congress including Minority Leader Nancy Pelosi (D-CA), Rep. Mike Honda (D-CA), Rep. Robert T. Matsui (D-CA), and David Wu (D-OR) also publicly denounced Coble's assertions. Pelosi described her colleague's comment as turning a historical "injustice into a virtue." Said Rep. Pelosi, "His remarks demonstrated an appalling disregard for civil liberties and inexcusable ignorance of history."

A mildly repentant Howard Coble subsequently issued a tepid apology stating that the decision by President Roosevelt to intern Japanese Americans "was in fact the wrong decision and an action that should never be repeated." Coble, however, declined to step down as chair of this key congressional subcommittee, leaving many to wonder whether the authority of his prejudices will further compromise the rights of those individuals and groups held under suspicion during the current reign of US government terror justified under the pretext of "protecting" its citizens.

The reader should know that the events and experiences recounted in *Blossoms in the Desert* are neither a departure from the course of US history nor an aberration in its unjust targeting of an entire group based upon race. Indeed, the concentration camps erected for Japanese Americans and the government agencies responsible for administering this domestic gulag sprang out of the same bureaucratic regime that had developed the network of "reservations" that held Native Americans who had survived extermination or forced removal from their homeland. This model of civilian surveillance and control later was exported by the US to South Vietnam in the form of euphemistically-named "protective hamlets" designed to save the people from themselves. Today, few know that a system of detention facilities across the nation is maintained by the Federal Emergency Management Agency (FEMA) in the event of widespread civil disorder.

The USA Patriot Act, rushed through Congress only forty-five days after the 9/11 terror attacks, represents the most recent threat to civil liberties as enshrined in the US

Constitution. In waging war against "domestic terrorism," government institutions and law enforcement agencies have been given broad powers in installing and maintaining a comprehensive system of social and political control more extensive and total than anything ever imagined by George Orwell. Already, thousands have been detained for indeterminate periods of time as mandated by the Patriot Act. One such individual is Pakistani immigrant Ansar Mahmood, who is due for deportation by the Federal Bureau of Immigration and Customs Enforcement after having been held almost two years after the events of 9/11.

As the stories that follow will show, that an entire class of people defined by racial identity can be stripped of their civil liberties and have their lives irrevocably harmed reveals American democracy to be more of an ideal than a reality. These accounts also alert us to the politically repressive measures already taken by the State in the aftermath of 9/11. The question remains whether this time around Americans of good faith will rise to the present challenge of anti-democratic governmental policies and practices.

— Darrell Y. Hamamoto
Sacramento, California

BRIEF CHRONOLOGY

December 7, 1941	Pearl Harbor in the U.S. Territory of Hawaii is attacked by Japanese military forces. War is declared against Japan the following day.
February 19, 1942	President Franklin D. Roosevelt issues Executive Order 9066 which bars Japanese Americans from the Western region of the U.S.
March 24–November 3, 1942	Approximately 120,000 Japanese Americans removed from West Coast and sent to detention centers and then concentration camps in California, Arizona, Arkansas, Idaho, Wyoming, Colorado, and Utah.
September 11, 1942	"Central Utah WRA Relocation Center" (Topaz) opened.
April 11, 1943	James Hatsuaki Wakasa shot and killed by soldier at Topaz.
September 1943	"Loyalty Oath" dissenters from Topaz numbering 1,459 sent to Tule Lake segregation center.
June 1, 1945	Topaz High School Class of 1945 graduation ceremony.
September 2, 1945	Japan formally surrenders to US ending World War II.
October 31, 1945	Central Utah WRA Relocation Center closed.
August 1, 1970	First reunion Topaz High School Class of '45. Miyako Hotel. San Francisco, California.
January 2, 1974	Central Utah WRA Relocation Center placed on National Register of Historic Places.

February 19, 1976	President Gerald Ford rescinds Executive Order 9066.
November 25, 1978	First "Day of Remembrance" held in Puyallup, Washington.
August 2, 1979	Sen. Daniel Inouye and Sen. Spark Matsunaga introduce S. 1647 Commission on Wartime Relocation and Internment of Civilians Act (CWRIC).
July 31, 1980	President Jimmy Carter signs CWRIC into law.
August 10, 1988	President Ronald Reagan signs Civil Liberties Act into law.
October 9, 1990	Reparations payments begin disbursement.
September 27, 1992	President George H. W. Bush signs H.R. 4551 into law providing reparations to former internees left out of original disbursement.
May 29-30, 1993	"Return to Topaz." Four hundred former Topaz residents visit site.
August 19–20, 1995	Fiftieth anniversary reunion, Topaz High School Class of '45. Miyako Hotel. San Francisco, California.
August 31, 2002	All-Topaz Camp reunion. Miyako Hotel. San Francisco, California. Topaz High School Class of 1945 57th reunion dinner.
February 4, 2003	Congressman Howard Coble (R-North Carolina) on a radio program justifies the internment of Japanese Americans during World War II, causing diverse Asian American civil rights organizations to call for his resignation as Chair of the Subcommittee on Crime, Terrorism.
September 6, 2003	Publication date of *Blossoms in the Desert*.

ISAO BABA

Current Residence: San Jose, California
Prewar Residence: Warm Springs, California

We lived in Mission San Jose—actually Warm Springs—where we farmed until we were evacuated. I was a freshman at Washington High School in 1942. Most of the kids were Caucasians, Portuguese, Italians. Some Chinese, some Japanese.

On December 7th, I wasn't scared or ashamed. I didn't think too much of it. My grandfather was arrested the next day and was taken to an Oakland jail. My father didn't want him to go alone because he had some difficulty understanding English, so he volunteered to go along with him. From Oakland, they went to Sharp Park, California, and then to Crystal City, Texas, and then to Santa Fe Detention Camp in New Mexico. They were there until 1944, when they joined us in Topaz.

We were assigned to Block 9 and had two rooms, A and B. My uncles made some furniture somehow. The women were in one big room and the men had the small room. At first we ate together, but as we made friends we ate with our friends. That was probably the start of the family structure falling apart.

There weren't many Japanese kids at Washington High in Warm Springs and I got along well with all of the Caucasians. But it was no problem making friends in the new environment. I got along well with everybody. It was probably easier making friends in Topaz because everyone was Japanese.

I remember the dances at Topaz. I used to go to all of them at the high school. I don't remember the refreshments or the decorations. I was more interested in looking at the girls. I don't recall anyone having sex. I guess we were too young. Got my sex education when I went into the Army. I didn't have any dates in camp. I just went to the dances and met the girls there. We had a gang of about ten guys and we would talk about the girls. Some of the guys would have crushes on girls, but that was about it. There was one fellow in the gang, Tak Yanagi— he liked to talk about the girls, but he was very shy about asking any gals out.

I learned how to smoke in camp. In the rec hall, somehow we made a hole in the floor and made sort of a cellar there where we used to hang out. We would go down there and smoke Bull Durham. I don't know who got the tobacco, but I got to be pretty good at rolling them. We didn't smoke steadily, but we would do it often enough. I started to smoke regularly when I went into the Army.

For me, the camp education was sufficient. I didn't have any ambitions to go to college. I went to a mechanic's trade school. I can't say that I was bitter about the internment at the time. Later on, I didn't think it was right. I didn't have any apprehensions about coming back to Warm Springs, but I was young and not much bothered me at the time. By the time I came back—after my Army time—everything was rather quiet. The only good thing that came out of the internment experience was that I made a lot of friends. Other than that, nothing. I think the reparations were good, but it was not enough and too late in coming. The older people did not benefit at all from it.

Siberius Saito

PAUL BELL

Current Residence: State College, Pennsylvania
Prewar Residence: Berkeley, California

After my graduation from junior high school, Dad informed us that he no longer had a job, that the government was diverting its budget for his office into the war effort. He got a lead that the government was looking for agricultural directors for the War Relocation Authority. He interviewed and was offered the job in Central Utah at Topaz. My parents believed that the government was not serving its citizens well by the internment, so this was an opportunity for us to try to help the victims through their ordeal.

After staff housing was built, we moved to an apartment where the folks and Gordon and Wini stayed, while Ernie and I lived in the men's dorm. It was convenient in that we had our own Pullman kitchen with refrigerator and electric range. There was a davenport, dining table, bathroom, and a double bed. That move was sad for me, because already we staff had so many advantages. We now lived in special accommodations in a separate section of camp. After I got reprimanded for letting one of my internee friends use the pool table in our recreation room, it was clear that the staff housing area was part of an intentional segregation policy. My parents even took some flak about inviting the Tatsuno family, Rosie Kumekawa, and *Nikkei* farm workers over to our apartment for sit-down dinners with a tablecloth.

At Topaz High the dances were one of the focal points. We spent all that time developing those fantastic crepe-paper decorations with romantic lighting, collecting the records, being there at the dance, and then cleaning up so quickly after the dance so that the Protestant church could have service in the hall the next morning. I struggled to reconcile the investment of time and money in decorations only to have them all torn down so quickly, but we really did need the visual escape from camp drabness offered by the decorations and atmosphere.

To date or not to date? Mom told me that it was a gentlemanly thing to take girls to the dances. But I shouldn't get serious with any of the *Nisei* girls because on the outside, attitudes toward mixed-race couples and their offspring was a tough road. I don't know how they did it, but she had sort of an understanding with the girls' parents that I would be no part of serious dating. Anyway, it was a relief to me, because nothing was expected other than to take another girl for an evening at the dance. I felt it was my job to book my date up with as many cool guys as possible. And with my school committee and sports connections, I could usually fill the bid pretty well. I also tried to keep the girl at arm's length to avoid body contact, even during the slow last dances. So, I only took one gal twice; the rest were all one-time-only events. Oh sure, there were some gals that I really liked, but I doubt that they knew it.

Rosie Kumekawa, Yas Furuya, and Dwight Nishimura "helped" me ask for dates. We would be walking by a barracks, and they'd ask if I had a date yet. If the answer was negative, one would walk up to a girl's door, knock and say, "Paul wants to speak with you," after which I would dutifully ask if she wanted to go to the upcoming dance with me. I was always surprised when "yes" was the response, for I was no great dancer and considered myself an anomaly. Caucasian staff members pressed me to date Jean Sanford, and later, Gwen Anderson, but I suspected motives of bigotry and stiffened at any advice from adults anyway. I never dated either one of them.

A couple of the gals were considered "fast." I wondered what that meant, and how and where "fast" activities would occur. I have no knowledge of any sex taking place and, if it did, those persons would have to be very resourceful. There was one older student leader whom the Caucasian women thought was such a nice boy, but none of the guys would have much to do with him. He was a good student, articulate, enjoyed classical music, had all of the social graces, and seemed like a good role model. Then one day he made overtures that I now would label as homosexual, but in those days I had no understanding of that phenomenon.

Experiences with the *Rambler* student newspaper were great, partially because we were allowed to work late at night to get the next issue out. I can still smell the odor of mimeo masters and correction fluid. It is amazing to me that we were given access to an office, a typewriter, supplies, and the mimeo machine to use day and night, sometimes without supervision. Our teachers were excellent in that they taught us how to be responsible in what we wrote. We had a constant debate about the fine line between gossip and social news.

The *Ramblings* yearbook was another exceptional experience. The creativeness in designing the publication itself, hammering out compromises between our dream and reality, and all of the many fund-raising activities to keep the cost to students low, all were meaningful experiences. Those carnivals, movies, and other fundraisers served as a community service involving the whole camp, and we took some pride in that. I can still taste those snow cones, hear the audience cheers for the heroes and boos for the villains during the war movies. During our planning, all sorts of setbacks and missed deadlines frustrated us (but probably built character). One such time, Mickey Suzuki exploded with a smash to the wall. The hole in the sheet rock was there for some time and we were fearful that our privileges would be taken away. It didn't happen.

Students were definitely involved in the camp and world issues beyond high school sorts of concerns. For

Ramblings Yearbook Staff

one of these, and I cannot remember whether it was the guard shooting an elderly man, the draft, or the signing of the loyalty questions, we students were planning a strike. At the eleventh hour, some of the faculty convinced our leaders that there were more concrete and positive things we could do, and the strike was averted.

Life at Topaz High was stimulating, but I always felt like an outsider. I couldn't have a GI issue Navy pea coat. My mom didn't knit, so I had no argyle socks. My pants were always too short, and we never did buy real Levi's. My hair was light and wavy, not black and straight like all the cool guys. I didn't tan; I burned. I couldn't jitterbug. My attempts at learning Japanese were a disaster, and my judo class experiences were visions of the room flying around as the wee *sensei* illustrated throws with my body. I enjoyed the May kite festivals and the creative designs by the little guys (and probably their fathers). I also remember the sounds of that Japanese music, turned up to high volume, that celebrated block bingo parties, and wondered how the older men could find something to get drunk with. Winter pounding of rice into what would become *o mochi* was memorable, as was the delicious taste of it hot out of the Dutch ovens heated atop the pot bellied stoves. Then there were the *Sumo* matches, unbelievable athleticism for such big guys. In winter the recreation fields were filled with water from fire hoses and frozen to become ice skating ponds. And the mud brawl with (against) faculty including those who were beloved and those not so well liked.

Finally, we graduated and I was glad to have a diploma. I worked for three weeks for the WRA assuring that the baggage of persons leaving camp made it onto the train.

Then it was my time to leave. My family had left for a trip to see my grandparents, so I had an all night party at our apartment with some of my classmates, who then rode illegally in the staff car to the train for a 4:30 AM departure. I hated to leave friends behind and wondered if I would ever see any of them again.

During the years when political action for redress was at a high point, I felt torn. I believed a wrong had been done and I knew the importance of the government acknowledging this wrong. But my role in life had been toward conciliation rather than confrontation. So I was for my classmates in their effort, but didn't feel free to join them in their efforts. I am glad redress came about, and I was sorry that it had not been in time to benefit the older folks who suffered such devastating loss. But I still have the nagging feeling that I was disloyal to my classmates during the process.

I carry some values learned in Topaz: An individual *can* make a whale of a difference. And we had a number of people, staff and evacuees, who are models of that principle for me. Respect for elders, for the family name and traditions, and for other people generally all became firm as the *Issei* contribution to the way I think about things. The place of the arts in maintaining dignity during hard times was realized during Topaz. The importance of education in self-realization became an important lifetime commitment for me. But mostly, the residents of Topaz, many of whom thought of themselves as merely ordinary folks, demonstrated the human spirit of taking whatever life dealt them and making something good happen out of that experience. What a rich legacy my Topaz friends have given me.

RAM-BLER

Vol. IV   No. 7   TOPAZ CITY HIGH SCHOOL   Friday, January 19, 1945

Commencement Exercises to be Held

Doami Chosen Senior Class President; Other Class Officers Revealed

In a spirited election for class officers held the first week of Jan., Junji Doami was elected as Senior Class President for the coming term. Other officers are: Vice President high senior, Betty Hayashi; low senior, Dorothy Harada; Secretary, Amy Hironaka; Treasurer, Harry Kawabata.

Junior class election return showed that Hid Kashima was chosen for the office of presidency. Others holding office are: Vice President high junior, Nancy Takahashi, low junior, Amy Tamaki; Secretary-Treasurer, Mihoko Shimizu.

Sophomores elected for their President, Ken Sato; Vice President high sophomore, Tak Eshima, low sophomore, Grace Mori. Secretary-Treasurer Sallie Tsugawa.

Baccalaureate Services Held

The Baccalaureate service for the graduating seniors was observ-

Senior Prom A Gala Affair

Considered the most spectacular student event of the year, the gala Senior Ball was held in the auditorium last Wednesday night with approximately 100 couples in attendance. Ichiro Ozawa, class president, was master of ceremonies.

Following the theme of "Blue Flame", the ball gave an atmosphere of soft lights, cozy tables, and chaise longues placed at strategic points.

In charge of the social event, the high spot c.' the senior calendar, were chairman Toshiaki Sakaguchi, and the following committees: general arrangements, Joe Suyemoto, Juro Hayashida; decorations, Ich Ozawa,Tak Doi,Junji Doami,Shiz Namba; refreshments, Elsie Itashiki, Mud Shinoda, Clara Mabuchi, Betty Hayashi, Sadame Hara, Alice Tsujisaka; Records and PA system, Seiko Akahoshi, Tubby Yoshida, Wacky Sumimoto.

The patrons and patronesses for the evening were Miss Eleanor Gerard, Mr. Emil Sekerak, Dr. Legrande Noble, and Dr. Laverne

Financial Help Offered To Graduates

To give financial assistance to 1945 graduates of January and June intending to attend college, a Student Aid Scholarship Fund will be established through the support of the center residents, it was announced.

1. Applicants may file applications for the grant two months before contemplated graduation, but no later than two months after the graduation date.

2. Assistance will be granted in order of approvals, but the student must enter a college or university before a period of ten months elapses after his graduation. Otherwise his approval for grant will automatically become invalid. In such an instance a renewal of application is required, subject to approval of the committee. Very special circumstances only will be recognized by the committee for reapproval.

All students planning to apply for these grants may see Mr. Sasato Yamate at Rec. 26.

Senior Week Observed

39 Students To Graduate Tonight

With "Beyond the Horizon" as the theme, the high school commencement exercises will be held tonight, January 19, at 7:30 P.M. at the civic auditorium. This event climaxes a week of senior activities and marks the fourth graduation exercise to be held at Topaz.

The public is cordially invited to attend the graduation ceremony.

PROGRAM

Processional.........Class of Jan. 1945
Pledge of Allegiance..........Led by
Elsie Itashiki (Chairman)
National Anthem....Graduates and Audience
Invocation..........Reverend Shimada
Welcome..................Elsie Itashiki
"We Would Be Building"..Graduates
"Beyond The Horizon"..Takeko Doi
Ichiro Ozawa
Piano Solo..............Keiko Kanzaki
Vocal Solo.............Elsie Itashiki
Presentation of Class...Dr. Laverne Bane
Presentation of Diplomas...........
Sup't L. G. Noble
Address to Graduates............
Project Director L.T. Hoffman
"Farewell Topaz High"..Graduates

The Baccalaureate service for the graduating seniors was observed by the High Senior students last Sunday night at the high school dining hall. Takeko Doi served as chairman.

PROGRAM

Dr. LeGrande Noble
Superintendent of School Chairman
Organ Prelude   Miss Aiko Takita
Processional
Invocation (in Japanese)
Opening Hymn

rard, Mr. Emil Sekerak, Dr. Le-grande Noble, and Dr. Laverne Bane.

Scripture Reading The Rev. Ozaki
Vocal Solo Miss Florence Nagano
Introductory Remarks Dr. Noble
Word From City Council Chairman
                        Mas Narahara
Sermon   Rev. Nugent
Closing Hymn
Prayer   Father Stoeke
Benediction   Rev. Shimada
Organ Postlude   Miss Aiko Takita

Senior Week Observed

The High Seniors, under the chairmanship of John Miyagawa, observed Senior Week from January 14 to 19 in their last round of school activities.

The program commenced with Baccalaureate Exercises, Jan. 14, Chr. Takeko Doi; Senior Banquet, Jan. 15, Chr. Naomi Kitagawa; Senior Ball, Jan. 17, Chr. Toshiaki Sakaguchi and Commencement Exercises, Jan. 19, Chr. Elsie Itashiki.

Presenting the 1944 Rams . . .

Presenting the 1944 edition of the fighting Topaz Rams. Left to right, Top Row: Mgr. Chiharu Kukokawa, Coach Mike Yoshimine, Coach Sam Yamamoto, Mickey Taaka, Mac Kato, Mike Hananouchi, Togo Oshima, Kei Nakano, Tak Inouye, Sus Iwasa, "Joker" Hada, Roy Kawemura, Mickey Suzuki, Coach Yosh Takakuwa.
Middle Row: Paul Bell, Juro Hayashida, Shig Omori, Chet Morizono, "Chuck" Yamasaki, Bill Ogo, Ich Ozawa, Tats Sano, George Okawachi, Sei Hirose, Mgr. Tubby Yoshida, Head Mgr. Clem Nakai.
Front Row: Tak Yago, Tak Eshima, Bob Utsumi, Tom Okai, "Jaydee" Doami, "Wacky" Sumimoto, Dick Katayanagi, "JoJo" Kimura, Gus Sonoda.

Project Director L.T. Hoffman "Farewell Topaz High"....Graduates Recessional..Graduates of Jan. 1945

GRADUATES

Akiyoshi, Sumiye; Doi, Takeko; Endow, Tomiko; Furuya, Yasumitsu. Hayashida, Juro; Hitomi, Teruko; Ikeda, Natsu; Ishihara, Shigeru; Itashiki, Elsie; Kaneko, Teruko; Kanzaki, Keiko; Kashiwabara, Shizuko. Katayama, Tomoye; Kinoshita, Sachiko; Kitagawa, Naomi; Mabuchi, Clara; Maruyama, Asako; Miyagawa, John; Nao, Kazu; Osugi, Emily. Ozawa, Ichiro; Sakaguchi Masaaki; Sakaguchi, Toshiaki; Sato, Yaeko; Shimada, Harvey; Shinoda, Mariko; Suyemoto, Joe. Takahashi, Michiko; Takita, Aiko; Tamaki, Mary; Tamura, Lily; Yamate, Aileen; Yoshiura, Shizue; Otsuji, Fred; Shimada, Ellen. Tsugawa, Yumi; Nagano, Florence; Hirose, Lillian; and Nomura, Dorothy.

Club Election Returns Announced

Election returns from the various clubs and organizations gave the following as results:

HI-Y

President, Takara Inouye; Vice-President, Harry Kawabata; Secretary, Richard Yamashiro; Treasurer, Tubby Yoshida; Athletic Managers, Tats Sano and Togo Oshima.

HOME ECONOMICS

President, Lola Tsuchida; Vice-President, Kiyoko Ikenoyama; Secretary, Sadako Hamasaki; and Treasurer, Kikuye Hayashida.

CHORAL CLUB

Because of the conflicting schedule with other clubs, the Choral Club is disbanding next term.

BLOSSOMS IN THE DESERT   11

SEIKO AKAHOSHI BABA BRODBECK

Current Residence: Sacramento, California
Prewar Residence: Oakland, California

On December 7, I was at the movies with Daisy Uyeda and also Marty Oshima. The theater manager interrupted the movie and there was an announcement ordering soldiers to return to base. I don't remember the name of the movie but it was a matinee. We had to walk Daisy home because she was afraid of the dark. Then Marty and I headed for home, which was quite a distance.

We arrived in Topaz in September of 1943. We soon started school. As far as school is concerned, my mother and father said that school was my job. I enjoyed studying. No matter where I went, as long as there was a school I would just feel at home. The school really did not meet my challenge because the curriculum was not that complete. After I got to UC Berkeley, I could say that Topaz High did not prepare me for college. I could have had more science and math, particularly because I had picked science as a major. My feeling was that whatever they had to offer, take advantage of it, and if that was the best they could do, I said, "Well, use it." The teachers were trying very hard to teach, so I paid attention to what they had to say and made the most of it. I know I was a good student and I enjoyed the high school courses.

I've been active in school activities ever since grammar school through the eighth grade, very active in the class. I always held an office. I was an officer of the student body in junior high school. Being a joiner was just a natural thing for me. My mother and father were community minded. They felt one should participate in social activities and you should volunteer and help in so-called community affairs. Since my community was school, I always thought I should volunteer if there was a party or a dance, social event, stage play, or whatever kind of activities. I remember acting in school plays like *Andy Hardy*.

Most of my theatrical experience was really doing exhibition dancing. In Tule Lake they used to have these

Kazuko Hashiguchi Iwasaki

Memorabilia from Topaz High School Social Events

musicals, and I remember Yuki Shimoda who became a well-known actor was in Tule Lake, and he used to dance. He and an Okamoto girl used to teach us. I remember Natalie Nakamura [now Katayanagi] and I put on a cha-cha-cha rumba dance and my mother made costumes for us, and I later did jitterbugging.

I don't know where I learned to jitterbug; it just came naturally to me. I just did it and I could follow no matter who the partner was. There was no difference in the jitter-bug styles between Tule and Topaz. My brother was a good dancer. My brother was almost seven years older than me. He got to go dances in Tule Lake. My mother had a rule of sixteen or something for me. I didn't go on dates, but I went to the dances. My sister-in-law and my brother were very good dancers. I know that when I was at Cal even the Blacks would stop to watch me because I danced like a Black. It was instinctive except that there weren't that many Blacks at our grammar school. I could imitate and dance like a Black; I knew that.

I enjoyed dancing with Tubby Yoshida because we dated. I think we dated because we both enjoyed dancing and we both enjoyed school, too. Of course there was Wacky Sumimoto. Being from West Oakland he was a natural dancer. Funny thing, I really never knew Wacky that well before the war. The only times I would see him was at the Japanese movies that were shown at the Japanese churches or Japanese school halls. But when we got to camp, it was like kissing cousins. It was so natural. We were immediate friends. We have always gotten along like brother and sister. Even today, we can go two years with-out seeing each other and if I saw him tomorrow it would be like we had been seeing each other all the time.

For assembly programs, I would do exhibition dancing with Wacky on the stage. Tubby, Wacky, and I would choreograph the dances. Because when we were doing exhibitions, it wasn't just doing dancing. It was being thrown up in the air by Wacky, sliding between his legs. He flipped me over and he did handstands. We never did that on the regular dances. When you did exhibition dancing on the stage you had to do things a little differently. So Tubby, Wacky, and I would get together and decide what Wacky and I were going to do, and when we were going to do it. Tubby would take care of the music. We danced to "In the Mood" and other popular jitterbug music. I liked "Take the A Train" with Duke Ellington. The bands I liked to dance with were strictly the Big Band era like Artie Shaw, Tommy Dorsey, Benny Goodman.

My mother was a dressmaker, so she made me all-around pleated skirts. I had lots of them in all colors and fabrics. "Sloppy Joe" sweaters were popular in camp. They are pullover sweaters. You wore them large and they came down so low that only two or three inches of your skirt showed. There was a lady in our Block 10 who knitted, so I had handmade "Sloppy Joe" sweaters. I remember I had a dark green and one that was yellow that my mother had asked her to make for me. I remember wearing the pea coats that came down to our knees, and I always wore my skirts a little over my knees. The pea coats were government-issue from World War I and they were heavy because they were 100% wool. They were the "in" things. You wore these bulky sweaters and short skirts underneath. That was the uniform because everybody—children and adults alike—wore them. They were comfortable because you could wear anything under them. They were great.

I remember wearing white buck saddle shoes with bobby socks. I would keep these shoes clean by using a big powder puff dipped in white talc, which I pounded against my shoes to make sure they were always really, really white. It was my trademark. Boy, I remember pounding in that talc and stomping around to get rid of the excess powder. I don't remember where I bought my shoes. Mom used to teach pattern drafting for dressmaking and somehow or the other if I needed a new dress or outfit she would make it for me. I was lucky. In grammar school, if it was May Day and if I were going to do a folk dance, she would make me a new peasant skirt which had at least twice as much material so I could twirl around. She would whip up these garments the night before any event. It was a creative outlet for her.

Things happened so quickly for me to graduate early with the class of January 1945 that sometimes I can't remember the graduation activities. I do remember we wore caps and gowns and that everybody was going to wear high heels and I didn't have a pair of heels. Ets Honnami loaned me her heels and I wore them down the aisle and I was very appreciative for her doing that. I don't remember if we had a banquet or anything else because my early graduation was so totally unexpected. The first thing I knew, my mother made me several suits to wear in college. She also made me a bathrobe and she remembered that Tubby did not have a mother so she made a bathrobe for him, too.

CARVIN DOWKE

Current Residence: San Francisco, California
Prewar Residence: Centerville, California

My name is Carvin Dowke and I was born on February 21, 1928 in Centerville, California. I am the fourth of five children. My father raised chickens and was into truck farming in Centerville even though he studied to be a pharmacist. My mother was born in Hawaii, but she was raised like an *Issei*.

My parents did not talk very much about their backgrounds, so I don't know too much about them. I know that my father believed that Japanese were discriminated against, so I remember him always telling us that we had to be better than White people.

I was never a very good student but I do remember I asked my history teacher in camp why we were there. I told the teacher that we are learning about the Constitution and stuff and that the teacher was preaching this, but that they are not treating us in the way in which we were being taught.

I do remember playing sports and baseball. I don't know if I am the only one who pitched a no-hitter in Topaz, but that is what I remember. Sports is what kept us going in camp—something to distract your mind.

I really believe that it was my parents who suffered more than us. They had to haul all five of us children around. I believe that the *Nisei* and the *Issei* are close because we were taught a lot about the parent-and-child relationship. I think it was a good idea that we had both cultures. I remember that my parents had to sell this and that and move out when we were told that we had to move. At the last minute, we had to grab everything and get out. When we returned, there was nothing left. People just pilfered everything. I think the government gave us some money, but it was not enough to cover for the four years that we were cooped up in the camp. I believe that it was pretty rough.

Camp brought me close together with my parents and my schoolmates. We have this reunion thing today which makes us very, very close. I was the chairman of this group that we had. It is a lot of work, but you don't mind the work if everyone enjoys it. It is surprising to know that after fifty years we are still together. It is so surprising that when I send out a notice to go somewhere, I get replies immediately indicating that they want to go even though it may be months away. When things happen like that, you don't mind organizing things.

We had many people in our class that have accomplished many things. A couple of people joined the Air Force and came out colonels.

I left Topaz in 1945 by myself. I went to San Francisco and stayed at the San Francisco Buddhist Church. It was converted into a hostel then for people returning from camp. I took the bus to get there. My parents joined me in San Francisco later. I also was a schoolboy while going to school at City College. I was paid thirty dollars a month, which I thought was a lot considering I only was paid fifteen dollars a month in camp. Then I got drafted. I was scheduled to go overseas. The people that I trained with went overseas. Some never came back. It could have been me.

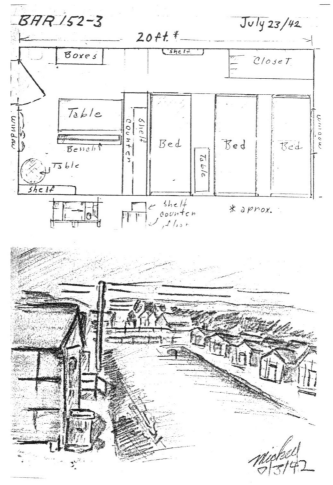

Mickey Mike Suzuki

Sketches of Tanforan Barracks

MITSUKO NAKAMIZO FUCHIGAMI

Current Residence: Romoland, California
Prewar Residence: San Francisco, California

W e were living in San Francisco where my father was a buyer for a major import/export company. Most of my friends were *Nikkei* and were attending Lowell High School. On Sunday, December 7th our family was at home and listening to the radio in shock and disbelief. Soon, we noticed FBI men on every corner and our neighbor was taken away. There was a military person standing at his front door with a bayonet on his rifle. It was very frightening. The next day at school, some of our classmates looked at the *Nikkei* students with suspicion and made us feel bad, though we knew in our hearts that we were loyal Americans.

After growing up in the mild climate of San Francisco, just the sight of the isolated and desolate location of Topaz was a great shock. Added to that was a dust storm that greeted us as we stepped from the old bus with the muffled noises made by the Boy Scout drum-and-bugle band as they tried to make us feel welcome. Again, we were processed and assigned our quarters. My uncle joined us and since there were seven of us, we were moved to another block where we had two adjoining rooms. Each room had a potbelly stove which we were glad to see, little knowing how much we would appreciate the warmth during the long, cold winters, *if* we could get coal which seemed to be in short supply in Block 42. I even stayed home from school on coal delivery days in order to get our allotment of coal and coal dust.

The high school teachers were recruited from among the camp college students and those who were dedicated educators from the outside. The teachers helped many of us keep abreast of the curriculum we would have followed on the outside although there was much to be desired in the way of supplies. When I left Topaz in April of my junior year, I didn't have any difficulty taking up my studies at my new high school so what I learned in Topaz turned out to be okay. However, it wasn't so easy to adjust to the unfriendly attitudes of my new classmates on the outside.

I can still recall the jingles on the radio commercials and the songs from the *Hit Parade*. When I hear the popular songs of that era, I am reminded of the talent shows too, when Goro Suzuki was MC. In camp or anywhere, we wanted to hear the mellow sounds of Glenn Miller, the jive music of Tommy Dorsey, and, of course, the crooner Bing Crosby, and Frank Sinatra. When we relocated to New York City, we were able to see some of the performers in person at the Radio City Music Hall.

I remember ordering clothing from the catalog from the Montgomery Ward catalog as well as things purchased at the co-op. Style was not as important as long wearing, comfort, and reasonable cost. My wardrobe consisted mainly of blouses, skirts, and sweaters. I remember the kerchiefs to protect against the elements. The Mackinaws used to rub the hair off the back of the head because the material was so coarse.

I guess I felt angry at having to give up the life we had before but *gaman* and *shikata ga nai* [philosophy of it cannot be helped] got us through all that we had to endure. I didn't talk too much about camp, but our discussions at the Cardiff reunion and this questionnaire is certainly bringing back a lot of memories. The most difficult time was our introduction to camp life in Tanforan when all of us were in one small room. Our family stayed together throughout camp days even to relocating as a group to New York. We almost always ate together. We didn't enjoy apple butter. I still don't like and will not eat tripe stew or anything like that. My parents always encouraged us to do our best, get a good education, work hard and hope for the best. They always said this is our country and we should be loyal. They became citizens as soon as the US allowed them to become American citizens.

I have attended almost all of our class reunions and I am glad to be a member of the class of '45. We all need to know we have choices and that's what we missed during evacuation and internment. When we again had choices of classes, sports, activities, choir, we enjoyed them. We formed a bond that continues to keep us coming back to reunions to be reminded of the happier days during those dark years behind barbed-wire fences.

WASCO AKITA FUJIWARA

Current Residence: The Dalles, Oregon
Prewar Residence: Dallesport, Washington

T he small Japanese American community of Dallesport in Washington and The Dalles in Oregon were evacuated to the Fresno Assembly Center in California in May of 1942. We lived in Dallesport and we moved into the Japanese school/community building for a couple of weeks because we had to leave from Oregon. Other families had friends or families to live with, but our family was so large and had no place to go, so we had to live in the community building. Several weeks later we took the train to Fresno.

It was a big trip for me. I had never been anywhere. Fresno Assembly Center was just a temporary camp. We stayed there about three months. We were then sent to the Tule Lake concentration camp because they had just finished that camp. We stayed there one year when they divided the "loyal" from the "disloyal." We moved again, this time to the Topaz, Utah camp.

When I think back to being uprooted from our home and sent way down to Fresno, I was scared. I didn't know anybody. It was a terrible shock. I can remember being the only girl in the family; my mother died when I was seven. So here I am, I'm the only girl and I had to fend for myself because the boys could not go into the girls' place.

But, of course, our family slept together in the one room that was assigned to them.

In camp, since I was the only girl, I had to do all the laundry using a washboard. I didn't get any help from my brothers. They were too busy playing. I was lost when I first went into camp because I didn't know anybody. Actually in Dallesport and The Dalles I knew only a few Japanese people. My friends were all Caucasian. All of these people went to Minidoka from Tule Lake. Not one of them went to Topaz. When we went to Topaz we were the only family that went there. It was very lonely.

I thought our education in Topaz was very good. You must remember that I came from a very small school. It's not like the city kids where you went to big schools. My whole high school had maybe forty students. So, Topaz High was a big improvement. It was difficult to keep up with the city students. It wasn't easy to get good grades there. There were so many bright kids. When Japanese kids are smart, they are very smart. It was very competitive. I was probably in the lower half of the class. There was nothing I could do about that. It was genetic.

The Tajimas were also in our block. We didn't run around together though. I used to run around with younger kids. One friend was Dolly Sakita. She and her brother were adopted, very unusual in those days. Another friend was a Grace Yoshizuka. She was only a sophomore, but she eventually married one of our senior classmates. She married Shiz Namba. Dolly, Grace, and I were in three different grades, but we stuck together. There were a lot of girls in our block, enough to have a girls' club. We met at the rec hall and every weekend we got together. Oh, we danced together. We had so much fun. To me, camp was a good interlude because I would have never had that opportunity back home.

I used to sew all my clothes in Topaz. There was a sewing machine in the block manager's office. Other things I would order from the Sears catalog. My older brother who was on the outside used to send me money so I could to buy clothes and other necessities. My father thought I should share the money with the family, but I told him, "I spent it all because I'm the one who asked brother to send me the money."

I did have one guy—he wasn't really a boyfriend. He wrote to me. I was one of those people who never went out. My father never allowed me to go out. I was very sheltered and had to stay home. But I did meet someone in my senior year. It was really not serious. He was a San Francisco boy. It was nothing serious, just friendship. I started to date about the second half of my senior year. Until then I had no social life at all. My dad was very, very strict. But you know, when you are a kid you'd like to have a lot of fun. Japanese people are not like *hakujin*, you can trust them. My friend and I weren't serious. I was just dating. I don't want to name any names. Just say I was dating several people. At least I had a little social life, so I was prepared or rather educated in camp.

I didn't date anyone who was popular. The guy I was dating was a very serious guy, but you know me. I wasn't serious. I was out just to have fun. At that time the guys were mostly good friends and it was fun to go out with them. Certainly nothing went on. I do think several of our classmates were serious about their friendships, but they didn't do "that thing." It was very innocent because there was no privacy in camp. We couldn't even go to the bathrooms because they were so well lit and lights were on all night. If anything had been going on, the *Issei* folks would have been down on them. They made sure everything was just right. The *Issei* did not let anything get by them. They made sure we were not harmed in any way and that we were safe. We left Topaz about the middle of August. As soon as the war was over, the administration had us out of there in a week or two.

I am a strong person. I take the responsibilities for the family. I do everything. My husband is going to be eighty-six. I didn't know what I was getting into when I married him. There were no Japanese people living around here and my dad wouldn't let me go anywhere. I just stayed home all the time and I didn't have a chance to meet anyone. In those days you did not marry a *hakujin*.

Siberius Saito

Horse Stable "Apartments"

YASUMITSU "YAS" FURUYA

Current Residence: San Francisco, California
Prewar Residence: Alameda, California

We had to leave Alameda after Pearl Harbor in late February. Alameda was declared a military zone and all enemy aliens had to move out. So rather than splitting up the family, we all moved together to my uncle's house in Menlo Park. My second brother, Sot, did not go into camp because he volunteered for the service. He went to Camp Shelby in Mississippi. He was there right from the beginning with the 442nd Regimental Combat Team. He was in the 232nd Engineers Company and was sent overseas for the duration of the war.

In Topaz, they first started assigning people beginning with Block 1. Later, either Block 1 or 2 was vacated for the Hawaii people who were sent to Topaz in 1943. I don't know the story why these Hawaiians were sent to Topaz. I remember it was the dead of winter and they did not have the appropriate clothes or shoes.

We had the three girls and we divided the room with blankets as dividers from the men's side. Later we acquired lumber, sheetrock, Masonite to make a permanent divider. The wooden crate that the potbelly stove came in was made into a couch, without cushions. It was about five feet long, sideways. My oldest brother and I made it. I remember that everything he started, I had to finish up. We made a stool and a dresser with four or five drawers. My brother bought a used table radio for about $5 before we went to camp. We received very clear transmission from St. Louis at around 11:00 PM to 12:00 midnight, but not nearby stations.

I was a sophomore when I went to Topaz. I went to school regularly, but I don't remember the names of the teachers. I was involved with school activities, but I will have to pull out the old yearbook to check this out because I don't remember all of them. I did work in two places— for the engineers doing topographic work outside the barbed-wire area and the other place was the hospital. I was an ambulance driver. I didn't have a driver's license. I was about sixteen years old then.

I heard lots of rumors. While I was there we were on the day shift and something happened at night with evidence remaining on the cots. I know his name but I don't know her name. We had two ambulances with two stretchers. The other one had seats to take care of outpatients. We had DOAs. You ever hear of the "death rattle"? Well, when we picked them up, we would hear this funny gurgling sound from the throat. I don't know how the people got to the hospital for an emergency. We had no training. No doctors, no nurses. We just drove when we got a call.

The Bells made it possible for us to comingle with them. Somehow or the other, when we were in Topaz, I was invited to the administration housing area for a party and I remember Paul was there, a couple of the teachers were there, and they had wine. Here I am and I'm only fifteen years old, and they give me a tumbler glass filled

Topaz Barracks

with wine. That's eight ounces. One glass went down easy, the second one went down easy. By that time I got giggly. One of the teachers was worse off than me and I had to escort her back to her dormitory. She wasn't too steady on her feet, so the only way I could hold her steady was to slide down the hall against the wall. I then went back to the party, went home, and everything I ate came up. My stomach didn't feel good. I was the only *Nisei* there. They were mostly teachers.

There was one teacher. What was his name? Mr. Peters? Well, this one teacher had his car there and he asked us out to a picnic in the hills. There were three or four of us. Later on, he was getting a little too chummy. He was looking for companionship at that time.

In high school, the different classes had dances in the school's mess hall. I was the disc jockey and the records belonged to several people who loaned them to us for the dances. We played music from Glenn Miller, Artie Shaw, Dinah Shore, and Frank Sinatra, but he came after the big bands started to fade. We wore sport clothes. Slacks and sport coats if you had them. But as DJ, I didn't have to date. Others had dates or went alone. We used to have punch made with jelly, but I don't recall what we had to eat.

We decorated the hall with crepe paper. We always had a teacher for a chaperone for the school dances. I knew how to do the fox trot, waltz, and jitterbug.

I never heard of any kind of hanky panky going on. Not at school, only the incident in the ambulance. The whole hospital heard about it. They heard that something

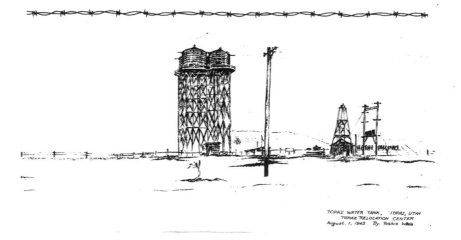

TOPAZ WATER TANK, TOPAZ, UTAH
TOPAZ RELOCATION CENTER
August. 1, 1943 By. Yoshio Wada

was going on. In Tanforan, too, there was something going on. It was hearsay. A little activity, one night, going on in the grandstand. It went a little further than that. I didn't actually see it. There was no privacy. If there was any sex going on among high school students, I didn't hear about it.

I climbed up the Topaz water tower. Seventy-five feet high, maybe higher. I went all the way up and crawled around the ledge. Going up was as bad as going down. You grabbed each rung very carefully. I went up with someone, but I forgot his name. Four water tanks on top. Made it look like one big one from afar. They were the biggest water tanks in Utah. I don't think too many guys went up there. It was just outside of the fence, on the east side, near Block 7.

I don't recall any riots in Topaz. In fact, I didn't know someone got shot until I read about it. [Mr. J. Wakasa who was walking his dog near the fence, inside the fence. He was shot in the back by one of the guards in the guard tower. The guard testified that he thought Wakasa was trying to escape. The soldier was acquitted of the crime and was transferred out of Topaz. —DUS]

I remember that trucks went up to Topaz Mountain to pick up gravel to line the roads in camp. There was one fellow who didn't come back. He wanted to commit suicide. They sent trucks to find him that night. They found him. He had hypothermia, but he survived.

I graduated in January, 1945. By the time our class was ready to graduate, there were only twenty of us left. To make it look like a nice, large class, we went down the aisle single file, rather than the traditional double file. The graduation service was held in the new gymnasium. Don't remember the speakers, but we did have caps and gowns. We ordered them from some company in Salt Lake. I did have to go to SLC to pick up the name cards, which were being made up for our class members. These cards were slipped into our graduation announcement. Since I was going to SLC for this assignment, I remember the teacher who was the pianist, Barbara Loomis, asked me to pick up the sheet music for "Pomp and Circumstance" for our graduation march. I believe the suit I had was ordered through the Spiegel mail order catalog that everyone had access to.

My legacy for my grandchildren would be one of the problems I had, which was being raised among Caucasians: I never thought of myself as Japanese. The drawback was that you could be with *Nisei*, but never fit in. I was always the "new kid on the block." I couldn't figure out why I didn't fit in. I had that problem in Alameda, Tanforan, and even in Topaz. I guess people thought I was cocky, but that's the way the *hakujin* and I were.

I'm not bitter about the internment. I was too young to think about that. When I reached Delta after leaving Tanforan, I felt that if my forefathers came to this country and survived, I could, too. I went back to Topaz on the "Return to Topaz tour in 1993," and went back again last year in 2001. There is nothing there. I saw remains of the foundations for mess hall and laundry room and plumbing fixtures. When I went back there again last year, I picked up half a skate and I couldn't figure out where the people skated. I left it there.

TAKUZO "ANDY" HANDA

Current Residence: San Jose, California
Prewar Residence: San Francisco, California

After December 7th, my parents took care of the evacuation. I have two older brothers and I just followed along. I don't remember any of the preparations. My parents had bought their house in my brother's name. You know Wayne Collins? He's an attorney. I think he took care of the house, collected rent, paid the mortgage, and watched the house. So we had a house to come home to at the end. I think this is what happened, but I'm not too sure of it

At Tanforan we lived in the horse stables. We had two stalls. There were eight of us, you know. We belonged to the "Blue Shirts." Each rec hall had a club and I went to the one where Maxie was and we all wore these plaid shirts from Montgomery Ward and we wore them inside out. We called ourselves the Blue Shirts. Who was there? Maxie

Sou's pant's Co.
Chicago, Ill.

Dear Sir:

   I am 17 years old, 5'6" tall and
an american citizen of Japanese descent
and I have heard that your firm is
hiring people to sit on benches to
test the durability of ~~your~~ pants.
   I have 17 years of experience in
this field and if you hire me I'm
sure you'll never regret it.
   Kindly inform me as soon
as possible of your intentions.

           Sincerely yours
           Andy Handa

and the old YMCA group: Joe Inatome, Bill Sakai. The old YMCA group, but they were a little older than me.

I don't remember the train ride to Topaz, except the Black porters wanted a tip. I can't remember where we ate. I just remember the Black porters wanting tips. Did I ever tell you that a number of years later—in the early 1970s when I was on a business trip flying to Florida—the pilot said that we were flying over Delta. I said, "What the hell. Why is he mentioning Delta?" Evidently, there is a radio beacon for planes in Delta and I looked out the window. Sure enough, I could see the outline of the camp streets! What a sight! What memories.

Kanger's name was Kengo and it changed to "Kanger." Do you know that they called me "Chu Berry"? We used to listen to Black jazz and there was a fat saxophone player named Chu Berry. Leon Berry was his name, but they used to call him Chu Berry. He played for Cab Calloway and we used to listen to him. One day, a group of us were walking down the street and we came across another group like us, the Chinatown Japanese. Guys that hung around like Tak Kubota, Skinny Gyotoku, and Masa Takatoshi. Remember him? He was kinda fat and chunky. Anyway, Harpy Komaru says, "Hey there, Chu Berry" and before you know it, they started calling me Chu Berry and I wasn't even fat.

You know how Chinky got his name? There was a cartoon character that was named "Chinky" who was tall and skinny. When Hank joined the Y, he was relatively tall and skinny, so we called him Chinky.

You bet, we'd go to the ballroom dances all of the time. I like to dance, actually. I liked to jitterbug. We used to listen to Black music: Duke Ellington, Count Basie. That kind of thing. "Moonlight Serenade." That's not Black. There's "One O'Clock Jump" and stuff like that. I used to go steady with someone. It started in Tanforan and in Topaz we still went around: Shigeko Suzawa. She passed away about four years ago.

In Topaz I worked at the Co-op as a soda jerk. I got syrup and added carbonated water. I got paid. It wasn't at the main canteen but near the Ad building. You know who got me the job? Tosh Kubokawa. He was running the store. He lived in our block.

I'm not bitter about the internment experience, unless I could get even. Gotta roll with the punches, the dirty White bastards. I told Daisy I read the Pacific Citizen. All they do is cry about the situation. Why don't they blow up FDR's tomb? He was a two-faced phony SOB. Go the way they think the public wants. No principles. The fact that the White bastards would pull shit like that does piss me off. In fact, when I see Tubby Yoshida, I'm going to tell him that when I started work at Lockheed, I did as little work as I could. I took as much money as I could. This is not to emulate my White colleagues. I'm just getting even with the goddamn government for the way they treated our parents.

JURO "JIGGS" HAYASHIDA

Current Residence: Hayward, California
Prewar Residence: Berkeley, California

In Berkeley, before the war, most of my friends were Japanese. I had a few Caucasian friends, but most of my activities centered around the Boy Scouts—which was all Japanese—and the church-sponsored sports games. I went to the Berkeley Methodist Church, which was all Japanese.

I don't particularly remember December 7th. I heard that Pearl Harbor was bombed. It was just news to me without any real emotion that I can remember. I was not afraid or ashamed. I was very naive about everything. Of course, it affected my parents a lot, but I just did whatever my parents told us to do. We were a very obedient family and whatever the authorities or our parents told us to do we did. That's the way Japanese people are: quiet and obedient. And my parents raised us that way. We were taught to respect our teachers, parents, laws; to live according to Christian principles; never bring shame on to the family. We knew that we were different from the rest of the population but felt no shame. My Caucasian friends were very nice and supportive and did not give me any difficulty. It was only after our return that I encountered

some disparaging remarks. At that age, we were very naive and didn't know too much about politics or think much
about losing our civil rights. We didn't discuss the situation at home and just went along with what the authorities said to do.

We heard a lot of rumors about Topaz and wondered
what kind of place we were going to. We got on the train
that had gaslights with the shades pulled way down. I
don't remember eating at all. We all sat together and I
remember crossing the Salt Flats in Utah. I didn't keep a
diary. In retrospect, I wish I had. I heard that Bob Utsumi's
mother kept a diary and I'm sure some of the girls did
also; they probably had lots of time.

We had a drum and bugle corps as part of the Boy
Scout troop from Berkeley, Troop 26. So whenever a new
group arrived on the bus from Delta, we welcomed them
with our drums and bugles. I played the drum and my
brother played a bugle. We wore our Boy Scout necker-
chiefs and shirts. I'm proud of that. There are some pictures of that somewhere in the archives.

When we first got there, we set up our beds and got
coal from the place near the latrine. My brothers were pretty
good carpenters, so we all looked for scrap lumber and
made furniture and partitions. In fact, I made a desk with
three drawers and a linoleum top. It was pretty nice and I
still have it! It is in our garage. Sort of stupid, but there
was some sentimental value to it and I brought it back
and was proud of it.

All of the students were able to participate in a lot
of activities at Topaz. I am not sure that I would have
been able to do as much at Berkeley High. It was so big

that I think I would have been lost. But who knows. At that time, most of the *Niseis* were quite and reserved, not very aggressive. It is certainly different now.

In the summer, I went out to Provo and Hinckley to pick fruit. We lived in a tent city. The farmer told us that if we picked fruit at the top of the trees we would get paid 35 cents an hour. But I said "no thanks" and got 25 cents an hour picking fruit at the lower elevation. But I thought that was pretty good. I made $2.50 per day. In town, I bought a brand new suit for $10. I will never forget that. In the tent city, I was the camp barber. I didn't get paid, but the fellows would get me a pie or something else good to cat.

In the small town of Reed, I first saw some Mexican field workers hanging around the tent city. They seemed lazy and shiftless, the stereotype of a Mexican worker. But since then, after coming back to California, I had the opportunity to work with Hispanics and found that they were just the opposite from the impression that I had in 1944. They saved their money to send back to Mexico and they worked hard. It sort of reminded me of our immigrant parents, who worked hard and saved their money.

I can remember some of the nicknames: There was Sambo, Joker, Clem, Blackie (George Murakami), and Harlem. Hisanori Sano was so dark so they called him "Harlem," but now he is known as Harlan. He was a real good athlete. I was called "Jiggs" from the Berkeley days, when I was a kid, maybe from Boy Scout days.

Some of the fellows had pegged pants. I never did have them, but Juji had them; that was Joker. He really surprised me. He was a clown in camp and then after he was in the Army and became a real thinker and scholar. Some of the fellows also sported hair styles—Hollywood style— that was combed back to look like a duck's rear-end and held in place with a lot of pomade. I wasn't that aggressive and didn't do anything out of the ordinary or risky.

I graduated from Topaz High in January 1945 and came back to Berkeley to go to UC. I'm not angry about the evacuation, but I know it was a big mistake. The people who were in power, the ones who made decisions, were discriminatory and they influenced others and it just grew. I get angrier now after all these years and as I find out more of the facts. The Arab Americans who are going through much of what we went through have a little different situation. The main difference is that they do not have the same roots as we did. As a group, on the whole, they would go back to the Middle East if they had a choice because their roots are deeper there. The *Nikkei* had their roots deep into America and would not have wanted to go to Japan.

I think there were some good things that came out of the evacuation. The country learned that there was a terrible injustice done to the *Nikkeis* and we had to suffer for it. But hopefully it won't happen again. It was a good experience for the country. It also opened up a lot of opportunities for the *Niseis*. The relocation allowed them to get better jobs instead of being gardeners and produce workers. It dispersed them all over the US and exposed them to another way of life and made them more mature.

Reparations was good, but it was just a token. It was a shame that our parents that suffered the most didn't benefit from it. For us young fellows, it was an adventure. There were a lot of things that I wish I could have done, like go back East to go to school. I think that would have been the best thing for me and maybe I would have finished college then. But I did the best with the breaks that I got and made the most of it. As I said, I met Tomoko, and that was good and I am happy with my life.

The Welcoming Band
10 a.m., October 1, 1942
Sumi on paper, 9 x 12 in.

In the dust storm there is the unforgettable music of welcome.

ROSE KAZUE ASOO HIRONAKA

Current Residence: Sacramento, California
Prewar Residence: Sacramento, California

My father was Lawrence Bunzo Asoo and mom was Haruye Asoo. My father was from Hiroshima prefecture in Japan, and my mother was from Okayama. My parents were married in Japan and they came over together to the United States. It must have been around 1917 or 1918. My dad's father was already in America and they had leased land for a fruit ranch in Walnut Grove, California.

After the crash in 1929, the farm did very poorly. In 1930 they moved to Sacramento. They grew vegetables for our own use: chicken and things like that sustained us. My father then worked for a nursery—Miyai Nursery—and he learned about plants. Then he started to do gardening work and he did that until evacuation. He did gardening even after he got back from the camps. As we got older, my mother did housework for other families after the war.

I went to Pacific Grammar School and then I attended California Junior High School. I was in the ninth grade when we were evacuated so I did not go to high school. Lincoln School was in the midtown Japanese area, but we lived in the country so we did not go to Lincoln. There were a number of Japanese families who went to our school and there were no Chinese, no Blacks, a few Spanish and Portuguese families. For junior high we went to the city as there was only one junior high school for everybody in the area. That's where I met Emi Yamada Masaki.

Sunday, December 7, 1941—Pearl Harbor Day—we were at home and we gathered around the radio to listen to the news. The next day we were hesitant to go to school as we were afraid, but we did go and we just felt that people were staring at us. There was nothing outwardly said or done to us, but on that day news was piped into our rooms that students should treat other students right and that the Japanese American people had nothing to do with the attack on Pearl Harbor. That made me feel more calm about the situation, and I think the other Japanese kids felt the same way. I did not feel threatened in any way. Things continued in the classroom like nothing was happening.

My folks were devout Tenrikyo members but, since the church did not have any activities for young people, we went to a Christian Church which was run by our Japanese school teacher. It was a Baptist Church. Reverend. Igarashi was the minister. Tenrikyo is considered more or less like Shinto religion. They had their church on Third Street in Sacramento. I recall going to the church but everything was conducted in Japanese and no one translated anything into English, so we just played around.

Along with the Florin area people, we were evacuated to the Arboga Assembly Center in Marysville. We lived south of the city proper so we were added on to the Florin-area people. We reported to some school in the town of Florin. The building could have been a packing shed or something like that. We were bussed to Arboga which I think was a bunch of buildings that were hastily constructed to house us. It was an open area with no trees; just a lot of barracks. There was a mess hall and I remember we always had to line up at assigned times. Our family was given two rooms and I remember the walls did not reach the ceilings so we could hear plenty from the family next door; all the fighting, the snoring. I remember it was very, very hot. We were there the latter part of May for several months when we were bussed to the train which took us to Tule Lake.

I remember the people who were lined up at the gate at Tule because people were curious to know who was coming into their camp. We felt like we were being examined. All of the Arbogo people were assigned to the same area. People from Florin, Placer, and South Sacramento were all assigned to the same ward; six blocks to a ward. It was in July or August. School started that fall.

I was in the sophomore class and I stayed one year in Tule. There was a Girl Reserves group I joined. There was a crafts class where we made paper flowers and jewelry out of shells that were found in the camps. I liked that.

My two older sisters wanted to leave camp right away so they both signed "Yes" to questions 27 and 28 of the Loyalty Oath. For some reason I had signed up, too, and I was only fifteen. That was unusual because I think one had to be seventeen years of age to sign that oath. I didn't know I had to sign that paper, but when I got a record of my files from the U.S. Archives, I saw a copy and I had written "Yes" to both questions.

My father said this was his adopted country so we should sign "Yes" to both questions because we were citizens of the U.S. He said we are going to have to live here and we are going to be faithful to the U.S. He said that Japan could not possibly win the war. He was one of the leaders in our camp. He went to the other areas to talk to the people and told them to think of the future and their children's future. People started to call him *inu* [spy] and other bad things. He said, "No, you cannot go along with a mob scene; you have to think about the future and be calm." We had some bad times about that. Some men folks would come to our house and try to talk my dad out of some of the things he was saying [that was pro-America], but he would not budge. They would get angry and start calling him *inu* again.

We were glad to get out of Tule Lake during the segregation period where the so-called "Disloyals" [those persons who voted "No-No", "No-Yes", or "Yes-No on Questions 27 and 28] from the other camps were sent to Tule, which became the Segregation Center, and the "Loyals" were transferred to the various other camps. We had signed up to go to the Amache, Colorado, camp as our first choice because we heard it was the best camp. However, we were sent to Topaz instead. Everyone wanted to go to Amache because there was no trouble there.

We didn't know what to expect, but we heard we would be okay. We lived in Block 39, way out at the other end of the camp. The Iharas were in the same block. Another Tulean in our block was Emi Yamada Masaki and that is why we always stuck together. School had already started at Topaz when we got there from Tule [late September of 1943]. I don't think we missed too much with our late start. I was in the same class as Tessie Sato Goi.

My favorite teacher was Mr. Maggiora. He was excellent. I thought very highly of him. He was very low key, but he helped us a lot. He was very kind, as numbers came very hard to me. I took bookkeeping from him. Miss Gerard was good and very helpful and she seemed to like the students. There was another teacher, an older woman, who [taught] social studies. She was very strict and demanded a lot from the students.

For some reason, one day all the students in the class walked out. I've never seen that done before. I said, "What are they doing?" We didn't know what the problem was, so the Tule people just stayed in their seats. The Topaz kids yelled out, "Come on out you Tule people!" We didn't know what was going on. "What are we supposed to do? Are we supposed to walk out, too?" Fortunately, the bell rang and we were really "saved by the bell." I asked, "What happened?" One kid said the teacher had called him a crummy name and he walked out, followed by the other kids. Maybe I would have walked out, too, if I knew what had happened.

Luckily, I had Emi to run around with, and gradually we got to meet the Topaz people like Kim Ihara, who was very nice. The people were friendly. One of the nicest Topazeans was Chiyo Date. She was so sweet and friendly and I remember her. She went out of her way to be nice to everyone. I had one class with her. I think it was algebra. I was friends with Mary Matsumoto and Ruby Ikeda. Mary Tsuchiya was always so nice to me, too.

I had a job with the Placement [Employment] Office; part time during the school year and full time during the summer. I was able to put my typing skills to good use. I had to fill out employment and separation forms. That's where I met Fudge Kawakami who later married Sam Sato. Sam lived in my block. He used to come to the office and flirt with Fudge. He was the driver for the bus that took people to and from Topaz to Delta. I thought he lived with his mom.

We wore cap and gowns for our graduation. I was on the committee to choose the commencement speaker. Miss Gerard was the advisor. Mary Iwaki was selected. She was shocked and said she couldn't do it and she was going to refuse. But Miss Gerard told her she would help her and knew that Mary could do a good job. She did a fabulous job as the speaker.

I remember in camp one of the girls got pregnant and they arranged for her to marry. They lived way out near the edge of the camp in the empty barracks. The people said she was naughty so that is why there was something wrong with her baby. The story was that the ear was not formed right. We were curious and wanted to see the baby, but she never brought the baby to the mother's house and we wanted to see the deformed ear. We said it was *bachi* [bad luck]. But we never got a glimpse of the baby. We were just curious.

We knew about the birds and the bees. Remember when Miss Muriel Matkin told us about that in health education or physiology. She was very verbal and outspoken, and she told us about the birds and bees, and she would draw all the organs on the flip chart and showed the penis and how the sperm got to the eggs. We were so embarrassed. I know we didn't have any books.

The Class of

Nineteen Hundred and Forty-five

Topaz City High School

Announces its

Commencement Exercises

Friday evening, June first

at seven-thirty o'clock

High School Auditorium

SHOJI HORIKOSHI

Current Residence: San Francisco, California
Prewar Residence: San Francisco, California

I attended Raphael Weill Elementary School, which is close by here in Japantown. I attended Roosevelt Junior High School. Some *Nikkei* classmates who went to Topaz were Tubby Yoshida, John Hada, and Joe Kimura. My friends were of mixed nationalities. I used to walk to Japantown. Initially, I attended church on Sundays—Christ Church. I went to Japanese school through my elementary school years at the Sano Japanese School located on Sutter Street, at the same site or next door to the JACL Building.

I sort of remember Pearl Harbor. On that particular morning that Pearl Harbor was attacked, I don't quite remember where I was, but I remember the newspaper vendors making their rounds yelling, "Extra! Extra!" I remember hearing that Pearl Harbor or the United States was attacked. I didn't know where Pearl Harbor was. It was early Sunday morning, and later on in the day, I put on my radio to see what was going on and heard that Japan had attacked the United States. My parents didn't say anything about the attack. Things were quiet.

At school the next day, I personally felt my schoolmates distancing themselves. They didn't say anything.

There was no eye-to-eye contact as I recall. Our neighbors were from different ethnic groups, but they never mentioned the attack on Pearl Harbor. They were friendly even until the time we left for camp.

After the announcement of Executive Order 9066 ordering the exclusion of Japanese Americans from the West Coast, we all got to talk to some of our friends to discuss what we were to do next. We prepared ourselves for a possible move to a camp. My parents proceeded to sell off equipment in their shop. We packed our personal belongings and gave some of the items away. We took what we could. We did store some boxes with my brother's friends. They must have been coworkers or people who were professionally associated with him. We didn't have a car. We rented our home.

Our family reported for removal to Topaz at the Kinmon Gakuen [Golden Gate Japanese School] on Bush Street. There were guards there. At the time, we were told to report to Kinmon. We were not living in that area, so to ensure that we would be included with those people and not be isolated from the rest of the Japanese community; we thought it would be better to move somewhere near other Japanese who lived in *Nihonmachi* [Japantown]. So we moved temporarily to the Aki Hotel. My parents took care of the packing. We were told to pack only what we could carry to the camp. We didn't know what was going to happen to us in the future. Perhaps even at that time I thought we had no rights in this country. My brother Shuichi was not with us then. He was at that time in Japan and he was working for the US government there. He was with the American Embassy.

When we first arrived at Tanforan, I knew it was going to be a racetrack because it was so reported in the newspapers and on the radio. It was quite an experience to hear that we were going to a racetrack and not knowing where we were going to stay. I guess we were processed somewhere underneath the grandstand and then somehow or another a guide took us toward the stables. We saw people walking, talking, and congregating near the grandstands, so I had a little curiosity as it looked like we were heading toward an area that looked like barns.

I wondered how living quarters were going to be constructed there. I saw some open doors and the beds in there looked like army cots and there were straw mattresses. I couldn't conceive sleeping on a straw mattress. Of course, it was smelly there. The floors were wooden but I think they painted the walls with very thin paint, like whitewash, and the odor of the horses was strong.

The latrine was quite an experience the first time I went there. There were sinks on one side and urinals on the other. In the center, there were some commodes which were separated by a five-foot wall which divided the seats into two sides with no partitions between them. We had showers. I think we had pull strings to release the water. We had a boiler system at each station.

For the trip to Topaz, we boarded a train on the outside of the camp where the San Francisco streetcars used to pass by to go to Daly City and to Colma, a very good system from Fifth and Market Streets. That was the back end of the facilities of Tanforan. The front side was the highway. I recall it was a railroad siding and that's where we took the train directly to Delta. They were regular passenger trains, apparently the old ones. Of course, they had guards at each section of the train. I believe they were armed. I don't remember going to the dining room. At night, we slept sitting upright on our coach seats. Nothing unusual happened on the train ride to Delta.

The train dropped us off at Delta, which was the closest town to Topaz. I believe it was a military bus that we boarded to go to Topaz. I thought Topaz was a big place, especially compared to Tanforan. I don't recall how or where we were processed. We had to carry the baggage to our new home. No one helped us. The weather that day was fine. It wasn't windy; it wasn't cold. We lived in Block 38, which is the back end of the camp. We had one room for the four of us. In our case, the rooms were completed. The walls were up, as was the ceiling. The one thing I thought was that the facilities were better here than in Tanforan. I never gave any thought as to how long we would stay here. I believed that this is where we would make our home for a while, but again, not knowing how long. I felt no anger about our incarceration at the time.

It so happened that our neighbors were from San Francisco. The Omi family had the next unit to us and we shared a common outside door. On the other side was my classmate Yuki Tsuchihashi's family. I think they relocated to the Denver area. Toward the end of the barracks was the Hagiwara family, who owned the Japanese Tea Garden in San Francisco. My father made a few pieces of furniture like a table, one chair with a back. Really bare essentials. The overall facilities were an improvement over Tanforan. The jurisdiction of the camps was by the government rather than the military and was much better.

There was no one particular teacher who mentored me. I remember Mrs. Lisle, and I think she was from Oregon or

Topaz High Assembly
(Clem and Joker at Microphone)

Washington. She always encouraged me to go outside the camp for school if I could. I think she taught English and social studies. We had the "core" system—which is a combination of English and history—and we got one unit of credit for this combination, not as two separate classes. This was a State of Utah mandate and I thought this was a very unusual concept.

I felt that some Caucasian teachers were good. A number of the internee teachers were great. Now Miss Watanabe, she was really great and taught her students well in geometry. Eiko Hosoi was very good, too. I think she taught English. Miss Watanabe was pals with another teacher—a Miss Sugihara who taught Spanish—and she was real good. They really knew their subject.

I went to the school assemblies and the only thing I remember is Clem and Joker, the comedy team. I thought they were like a professional team, as they were good. They had natural comedic talent, especially for Japanese Americans. I also attended church just once in a while. I never smoke, drank, or had sex in camp. I remember the water tower, but I never climbed it. We had a radio and the only program I really listened to was the *Hit Parade* on Saturday nights. I liked listening to Tommy Dorsey, Benny Goodman, and the Artie Shaw bands. When I left camp, whenever I had a chance, I used to go to Detroit to see all of those big bands.

I decided to leave Topaz after my junior year, when representatives from Michigan came to camp to recruit workers for the dormitories at the University of Michigan at Ann Arbor. Also, at that time, we asked if we could work there part-time during the summer and if there was the possibility of us working part-time during the school year. The response was positive and they gave us the opportunity and in that respect it meant that we had quarters in which to sleep and also the dining room where we could eat. So that meant I could go to school and have spending money.

Looking back on the incarceration, I thought it was rather unfortunate. We didn't have much power as a group. The unfortunate part is that we were incarcerated without due process. Having been incarcerated, you think more about the civil rights of everyone like what is happening today to the Muslims and the Arabs. Prejudice and discrimination still exist in this country.

KIKUKO NAKAGIRI ISHIDA

Current Residence: Pacifica, California
Prewar Residence: Medford, Oregon

We were horrified about the bombing at Pearl Harbor. Ada and I were on our way to a movie theater. Actually we were kind of afraid to go. I can remember in school on Monday our English teacher had brought a radio and we listened to the president. I don't know if that was the day he declared war but it was very trying. It was very scary for us. I felt sorry for my father. Since he ran a restaurant he usually was open until midnight, but he had to close up and we had to be home by 8:00 PM. And there were posted signs saying where we couldn't go. It made you feel almost like a criminal.

I can remember going home from the restaurant and packing our mom's china in newspaper and boxes. We were so fortunate we had this family friend who stored our possessions. We went directly from Medford, Oregon to Tule Lake in a Greyhound bus. There were so few of us. We had heard before camp days that Sacramento girls were going to be there. People from Sacramento—and the girls—were so tough. I guess they wore jeans. We wore pedal pushers. I hated being searched. Our belongings were searched by the soldiers. They went through all our belongings. The place was so desolate, all the stark barracks, just row after row. We were not the first ones in Tule Lake. I think people from Portland and Salem were there. We were in Block 14-16 and I forget the number of the apartment.

We were in Tule Lake from June 1942 and I don't remember the day we went to Topaz. I guess we had to write our choices and I don't know why we chose Topaz. Topaz was smaller, because there were 15,000 of us in Tule. It was fun to walk around the outskirts. One section we called "Alaska," because it was so far away. I think the rooms were like Tule. It was a good thing my dad was very handy because he made a big closet to separate his room from our room. He made bunk beds for my sister and myself. My brother had a cot outside in the so-called living room.

I think I enjoyed the chorus the most. We went to the church and belonged to the choir in church. In Tule Lake we joined the church choir and we had this wonderful gal, Helen Maeda from Washington. We actually performed the "Hallelujah Chorus." Oh, it was fun!

There must have been a notice or a call for volunteers or something to be a nurse's aide, so I applied. I guess Ellen (Shimada Shimasaki) and I went. We must have gone together because we lived right across the barracks. I remember the *hakujiner* nurse, a very stern looking lady, instructing us. There was so much to learn. I was a junior so I must have been seventeen. I'll never forget seeing this one patient. She was a mother, an older lady. I'd say she was maybe fifty and she had a tremendous stroke. All she could move were her eyes. Obviously she could eat because her daughter came and fed her every meal and took care of her. But just her eyes were alive. She wanted to say so much and all she could do was through her eyes. And I thought, "Oh, gosh." It was really something.

I can remember working on the TB ward. When you left the ward you had to spray the soles of your shoes with Lysol. I remember in one of the wards there was a tonsillectomy and I guess the child started bleeding, so I had to run to surgery and get Dr. [James] Goto. That was scary. The kid was okay. I can remember a couple of dances we went to at the hospital. That was fun. Dr. Sugiyama and his wife came. It was a staff party. I can remember Howard Mizuhara.

What's upsetting to me about the internment is that so many people don't know this happened. When I went to school in Milwaukee and I went home with one of my classmates up to northern Wisconsin, I stopped traffic walking the streets with her. They'd never seen a Japanese or an Oriental, I guess. I literally stopped traffic. Of course my classmates didn't know about camp. I could not believe it.

I wanted to add something about Jean Sanford. My sister somehow knew that Jean was attending class the following day, and she was going to be in my class. So she asked me to approach her and welcome her. Of course being *hakujiner* and we're all Buddhaheads, it would be difficult for her. So when I went to school and I saw her, I went up to her and talked to her. It was completely out of my nature, as I'm not that type of person. But she fitted in so beautifully. She was very active, a very bright girl.

She called me recently. She wanted to know of her background in camp. What she looked like. I had to tell her she was blond and kind of chubby and wore these

Oxford shoes. She said her mother made her wear them because they were good for her feet. I ran into her in Chicago in '48 or '49. She hadn't changed at all.

My best girlfriend, a classmate, didn't think that it was right for us to receive reparations. I admire her for saying it. It didn't change my feelings toward her. Yes, she was a *hakujiner*. I told her I wished my parents had received it, not us. It's too late.

Mickey Mike Suzuki

Tanforan Sketches

KUMIKO ISHIDA

Current Residence: San Mateo, California
Prewar Residence: Irvington, California

I don't remember details of the bombing of Pearl Harbor, but do recall the directives from the Civil Defense office regarding curfew and blackouts. There was an 8:00 PM curfew and everyone was to be confined to their homes until the following morning. I also remember my mother making black curtains to cover the windows so light wouldn't shine through during a blackout. It was an unsettling time, with the adults discussing the scary rumors about what was to become of us. My younger sister and I were not included in these discussions, but the undercurrent of anxiety and fear of the unknown was very disquieting.

The heat that met us when we got to Topaz was incredible! Everyone seemed to be wearing white shoes or boots. Later I found out that my shoes looked just like theirs. It was the powdery dust of the desert's sandy, clay-like soil that turned into blinding, painful sand, and dust storms that left a coating of dust on everything in the barracks room and classrooms. The dust and sandstorms made breathing so hard. We would tie our bandanas to cover our nose and mouth like bandits and hurry home as fast as we could. The other awful thing about the sandstorms was your legs would feel like they were being sand-blasted by the blowing sand. It was very painful!

Bathing was usually done late at night when the shower room was less crowded. I remember the cold winter nights walking back to the barracks after the warm bath. The *geta* would make crunching sounds breaking through the icy crystals of snow and frost. Mother devised a little innovation to protect our skin after our bath. She crocheted little woolen covers for our three metal door knobs (the outside door and the two leading to the rooms A and B) so our warm hands wouldn't have to touch the cold metal resulting in a piece of your skin being left on the doorknob.

The family as a unit was totally destroyed in the camp environment. Our lives as teenagers were ruled by peer standards. We ate as a group, attended school together, and all recreation and social activities were dominated by peer decisions and actions. Parental influence and control was lost under these mass-living conditions with no privacy or opportunity to function as a family unit. The children relished the freedom from parental authority, but it was devastating to the parents. My mother made efforts to keep us together by insisting that we eat as a family in the mess hall. I complained bitterly about how embarrassing this was, not to be able to eat with my friends. She then decided to get the food for all of us and bring it home for meals in our barracks room. (This didn't last very long either.) These were humiliating actions to a teenager and I resisted strenuously to all these efforts by my mother to keep her family together. By this time, my brothers were both drafted and in the Army. My older sister had left to go to New York to work. It must have been so painful for my mother to see her family slowly drifting apart.

One of the favorite outfits for the girls was to wear a man's white dress shirt over rolled-up jeans. Mother put her foot down about my younger sister and me wearing our brothers' shirts. She insisted that those shirts must be saved for when they returned from the service. So my sister and I were allowed only one shirt each. Over this outfit was the heavy pea coat which was the basic outer garment we all wore.

GREETINGS FROM TOPAZ

At the time, I was interested in a nursing career. So when the opportunity came up, I signed up to become a nurse's aide at the hospital. I think I was almost seventeen at the time. I don't remember the training too clearly, but I do remember we practiced giving injections by drawing a syringeful of water and shooting it into a lemon. The first real injection I had to give a patient was insulin to a diabetic. It was very nerve-wracking. I remember rubbing and rubbing her arm with the alcohol swab trying to work up courage to give her the injection. She kept saying, "It's okay, it's okay" to comfort and encourage me. Her skin was so tough from so many injections. I'm sure my shot must have been pretty painful.

One of the duties of the aides in charge of a shift was to count the narcotics locked in the drug cabinet. The off-duty aide and the incoming aide would go over the list together and count each controlled drug that was in the cabinet and initial each item listed. We were naive innocents who didn't know about illegal uses of these controlled substances. We just knew that these were pain relievers for cancer patients and other seriously ill people. It never occurred to us to experiment with the "medicine."

I also worked for a short while in the Isolation Ward, where the tuberculosis patients were housed. A gown and a mask were hung on the back of the door, which we put on when we entered a patient's room to care for them. We would remove the gown and mask and hang it back on the hook before leaving the room. This ward was removed from the general hospital wards and we had to walk down a long corridor to reach it. This meant walking past the morgue, which at night was so silent, dark, and spooky. I really dreaded that walk.

One very exciting part of being a nurse's aide was when I got to see the birth of two babies. The first time, I was just an observer. The second time I got to stand beside the mother's head and I was given two tasks. One was to give the mother a whiff of the ether when she had an especially painful contraction during delivery and the other was to check the time of the birth. When the mother had an especially strong contraction, I would soak the gauze and give her a whiff of the ether to help her over the worst of the pain. The mothers were conscious throughout the entire delivery. It was a shocking and an amazing experience for a naive seventeen-year-old who hadn't even seen a pet being born to witness the birth of a human being. I was so engrossed in the birth process I forgot to check the time of the baby's arrival! Fortunately, Dr. [James] Goto automatically checked the clock so I was forgiven for this oversight. It was truly an unforgettable experience!

There were some teachers I remember with fondness, but some of the teachers from the outside were not of the caliber we had in the California schools we left. Math is not one of my strong subjects, but Miss Hosoi—a fellow internee—made algebra understandable to me. She said math did not come easily to her, too, so she had to try lots of different approaches to find a solution. She was able to suggest different strategies to help us understand the problem. I think we had many outstanding teachers among the internees, none of whom had a teaching credential. Many of these internee teachers were college students themselves, who were teaching us the subjects they were majoring in.

I remember an incident that happened in a chemistry class. There was no lab or equipment, so the class con-

Topaz High Senior Girl Reserves

sisted of lectures and demonstrations of experiments. This particular day, an instructor—whose name I don't remember—was demonstrating how to heat things in a test tube. It was very important to heat the closed end so the gases can escape from the open end, he said. His demonstration was exactly the opposite and the heat built up in the test tube and it exploded. Since we were seated alphabetically, I was in the front row, and when I looked down on my skirt I found shards of glass on my lap!

The internment experience was traumatic for all of us, but I feel saddest for our parents. They struggled to provide for their families in spite of racial prejudice hardships. They faced obstacles so many times. Father was seventy years old and Mother was fifty-six years old when they were sent back to California to begin all over again in 1945. Two of their children were in the Army, two were in New York, and one child was still in high school. So this elderly couple who had nowhere to go was resettled at a dilapidated old house in San Lorenzo to work in a gardenia nursery until their sons came home in 1946 and the family settled in San Mateo. These elderly *Issei* are the people who should have been given the $20,000. They were the ones most in need of financial compensation at that time. The letter of apology and the check came too late for them.

About the bonding and the special relationships that have emerged from our camp experience: For three formative teenage years in high school we saw the same people at school, in recreational activities, in our blocks, at the co-op. These circumstances blossomed into the lasting friendships that continue for many of us to this day. Attending the reunions continue to reinforce these special relationships.

KENZO ISHIMARU

Current Residence: San Jose, California
Prewar Residence: Oakland, California

E ven at an early age, I can recall some of the boys—not my friends—calling me "Jappie" or "Japansie" and pulling the corner of their eyes to make it look slanted and narrow. I knew that I was different and it was that time in my life that I wish I was like the rest of my friends with Caucasian features. I was embarrassed of being Japanese and of my parents, who did not speak English well and did not participate in activities at school—although I can recall one time when my father did come to a Cub Scout event, a bean feed, and he was all by himself. I felt so sorry for him at the time. My father was the mainstay of the family and he instilled in us the pride of being Japanese. He would tell us that we were better than the rest and that we were smarter and that we had to work harder at everything that we did. It was difficult to assimilate or understand this at the time and I was torn between the Japanese and the White culture.

My only interaction with other Japanese was through the church. My father felt that since we were in America we should adopt a Western religion, so he sent us to the Sycamore Congregational Church in West Oakland, an all-Japanese church. We would get on a streetcar and go to

Broadway and transfer to another to 26th Street. That was the only Japanese contacts that I had until the evacuation.

December 7th, 1941, was a Sunday. I was at a church activity and on the way home I heard about Pearl Harbor. I was afraid and confused. I looked around at all of the passengers on the streetcar but avoided any eye contact. There were newsboys on the street yelling "Extra, extra." I did not know what to expect. I was filled with anxiety, but I went to school the next day. I cannot recall any ugly incidents. My Caucasian friends still played with me and the teachers were nice even as we discussed the event. I was ashamed of being Japanese as we listened to the declaration of war on the radio.

I remember that my father destroyed a lot of Japanese memorabilia. We didn't discuss the situation. We did what the authorities said to do. And when they posted a notice on the telephone pole close to our house telling us that we had to leave, we just left without any protest. As I look back on the events, I think what arrogant disregard the US government had on our civil rights and the humiliation of having a sign on a telephone pole like a "Most Wanted Criminal." My father left all the inventory of plants in the nursery and I often wondered whatever happened to it. We never discussed the situation. I can only surmise what it must have been like for him.

The train ride to Topaz was a long, tiring trip. We took forbidden peeks out of the windows that had its shades drawn. Beyond the Bay Area, we did not recognize anything. This was the first trip out of the state for all of us. I cannot remember eating, other than bologna sandwiches being passed out and receiving an orange when we stopped in the desert somewhere so we could stretch our legs. There was a cordon of military police surrounding us to make certain that we wouldn't escape.

I was anxious on the bus ride to Topaz from Delta. This was going to be our home for the duration. As we stepped off of the bus, we stepped into a powdery layer of talc-like dust that must have been three inches thick. I will never forget that. We were assigned to Block 13-4-E. For some fortuitous reason, we had a large room meant for six and there were only four of us. Papa fashioned a partition of sheets and made a bench or two. Mama was not happy. But this was to be our home for the next two years.

My time in Topaz is a fading memory. There was school that was hastily put together with teachers who for the most part were not qualified. I have tried to think of the teachers that I had. Eiko Hosoi taught math. And there was a Mr. Goertzel, who I remember because of his different-sounding name. I cannot recall any textbooks or homework or science experiments. School was a place where I had to go to and it was a place where we met our friends. It was the only activity in town. I think I may have erased a good portion of camp life from my memory because it was so bad.

I could recognize that the family structure was falling apart. My sister relocated to the East Coast after one year in camp. I no longer ate meals with my parents. When there was a vacant room in one of the barracks, a number of us young, rebellious fellows moved into it and set up housekeeping in the "bachelor pad." My father was the Block Manager and he did not protest too much and neither did the other parents in the block.

My father was getting concerned about my lackadaisical attitude about school. He always stressed education and felt strongly that I was not getting it at Topaz High. He applied for a position on the East Coast as a caretaker near New York, where my older sister had relocated. At the end of my junior year at Topaz High, we left for New York City with a train ticket and twenty-five dollars each. The train ride was a long one, sitting on hard bench seats with many soldiers on board. All of us were very apprehensive, but we arrived without any incidents. We stayed at a hostel in Brooklyn and a few days later a nice family came from Long Island, where my father was a caretaker and my mother was the cook. We had nice quarters, living on a large estate, eating decent food, and in a dust-free environment. But it was isolated in Sands Point, where the DuPonts and the Walkers lived. There was not much for a sixteen-year-old Japanese kid to do. I went to the big city—New York—where I stayed with my sister and found a job as a dishwasher at Toots Shors, a fancy restaurant. It was hot, steamy work, but a cook liked me and I ate very well. It was another adventure, but often it was a lonely one.

In August of 1944, a friend from Topaz, Sam Nakaso visited as he was on his way to New Haven where his sister was teaching Japanese in an Army program. We were in the same grade and he was going to continue his high school education in New Haven. He invited me to go with him to see New Haven. Since I had no plans where I would attend high school, I went with him. It was a nice school located on the Yale campus and I decided that I would join Sam in New Haven.

I found a room at the YMCA and worked at its bowling alley downstairs. I was able to support myself with a little help from my parents. After a season of dodging bowling pins, I felt that it was time to find a less hazardous job. I worked in a Jewish delicatessen, where I was exposed to bagels, cream cheese, lox, and kosher pickles. I learned to cut lox as thin as the Jewish proprietor. I was called "Kenzo the Rabbi" by my fellow worker—who happened to be Italian—because during Passover the proprietor asked me to stamp "kosher" on some of the packages so he could charge more for it.

School in New Haven was a different experience for boys from California. Everyone wore a coat and tie. There were few Asians but a lot of Black and Jewish students. There were many racial clashes between the races, but everyone accepted us. Sam was an exceptional athlete and he made many a headline with his athletic exploits. One headline that stands out is when he made the last-minute winning basket in a title game. The headline on the sports page read: "Little Jap Boy Does It Again." He was a very popular student.

In 1945, I had to register for the draft. I did not think too much of the idea that I would be going to be in the Army. Later that year, there was a program posted at the school that was offered by the Army Air Corps. If you passed the exam and passed the physical, you would be accepted into a flight-training program and you would become an officer and a pilot. My father did not like the idea, but he relented and signed the necessary papers. A number of us were being sworn in at the armory when the major in charge pulled me out of formation and led me into his office. He told me that the "Army Air Corps was not taking any Japanese, but maybe there will be another war." It was a devastating experience. Humiliated, I went back to my room in tears. The program was subsequently abandoned, but that experience stayed with me. Consequently, I did not tell the local draft board when I graduated from high school or that I had returned to California. I avoided the draft for four years during which time I graduated from college.

As I look back on the internment and incarceration and relocation, I get angry for the deprivation of our civil rights. I get angry for what my parents had to endure. I get angry over the racist politicians of the times. The facilities and food were barely adequate. The family structure disintegrated. On the other hand, I feel that for the most part the younger *Nisei* benefited from the experience. We were at an age where we had no material things to lose. We made a lot of Japanese friends and remain in contact with them even after all these years. We had the opportunity to participate in high school activities like student government, played on varsity sports teams, grew socially and went to dances, worked on the newspaper and yearbooks. Very few *Nisei* would have been able to do as much where they lived before the war. Many were exposed to the East Coast and the Midwest. We matured faster with more resolve and determination. One can only speculate as to what life would have been had we remained in California during the war years.

TOMIKO KUMAGAI IWAMOTO

Current Residence: Oakland, California
Prewar Residence: Alameda, California

I was at a basketball game on December 7th. The Bay Area had a tournament. They came from every city and competed against each other. They had the Berkeley *Nisseis*, the San Francisco Protos and Mikados, and we had an Alameda team. We had gone to a game in Alameda and I was coming home. The newsboys were saying that the Japanese had attacked the United States—I mean Hawaii—and there's a possibility of war. But I didn't think anything of it, but the folks knew. They had probably heard that Japan and America were getting into a disagreement and a possibility that there would be a war.

Going back to school was kind of hard. I had just started my freshman year at Alameda High School and all the Chinese were congregated together. We walked in and they had signs on them saying "I am Chinese." My Glee Club teacher said that all the Japanese children that are coming to school here are still your friends and we should not discriminate against them because it's not their fault. I remember I cried because I was the only Japanese girl in the class.

My father was arrested. All the people in Alameda were asked to leave because we were near the Naval Air Station. The people in Richmond were moving, too. I think they had a shipyard or something. That was on February 22nd, 1942. We were getting ready to move and my father was outside when these two FBI gentlemen came up to him and said, "Are you Kumagai-san?" They arrested my father without any questions or anything. They wouldn't even let my father shave. They followed him into the bathroom while he was changing his clothes. That was my first experience of my father being away. He went to Sharp Park. They had a detention jail or something like that. Then they sent him by train to Bismarck, North Dakota. He was there for a while and then after that he was transferred to Santa Fe, New Mexico. Then I think he went to Lordsburg, New Mexico after that. He was moved three or four times. He was gone for two years exactly; all during the time our family was in Tanforan and Topaz. Then two years later they said they didn't have anything against him, so they just returned him. That's a hardship that my mother went through, especially with my sister being mentally weak. That was really sad for her. She was about thirty-seven-years-old with these three children.

At Topaz High School we took some compulsory courses. But if you didn't like it you didn't study because we didn't care. It wasn't that important to us. But I enjoyed my shorthand class. I loved shorthand. First, I think I had Pearl Masuda. She was a real good teacher, but she was real strict. There was competition between the students. Fumi Saiki's older sister Yoshi was in my class and we would compete against each other. I hated social studies, but I loved physical ed.

In our block we used to have a team. An all-girls team. A volleyball and an all-girls softball team. We used to play against the old men in our block. The losers were supposed to purchase the ice cream. The old men folk would just automatically go get the ice cream because they knew the girls were stronger. My father was on the opposing team and he said they sure don't know how to play ball. My father was an avid baseball fan, so he knew exactly what to do and he used to try to coach them. But he said they were impossible. We used to have a good time. We had block teams, too. Do you remember Yosh Isono? Yosh Isono's team was from the next block. We were in 11 and they were in 12. I'm telling you, he would do all kinds of things. He would forfeit the game at the end, but say the girls got sick or something. He would tell us a lie and it wasn't a forfeit any more.

I told Mr. Maggiora when he was at our reunion how much I enjoyed learning from him. I think he really helped me pick up my skills. When I went to Merritt Business School I didn't have to do too much shorthand because I knew my ability was there. I remember we had this US history teacher, Mrs. Lyle. She was a real crabby lady and a little mischievous kid like Sab Shimomura was in our class. He would do the worst things in class. I can't remember what he did, but she would always get after him. But I think most of the kids were pretty well disciplined. She threatened to kick him out of the class. In camp he had a freak accident and lost a finger. After that he got kind of quiet.

I didn't feel like I was incarcerated at that time. What were we to think when we were twelve or thirteen? A lot of people are surprised that we don't hold it against the government. The head of the architectural department at Bechtel used to be one of my bosses. When I got the money he said, "The hell with the $20,000. You shouldn't have to pay any income tax and they should give you a lot more than $20,000 when they do that kind of thing to a human being." He was really mad about that. But I said, "It's okay. We got $20,000." But I felt bad for the parents because they were not able to receive anything. It was kind of late in coming. They needed it, but they still pulled themselves through even when they came back with almost nothing. I think it's the parents that we really should appreciate.

Barrack 152

Mickey Mike Suzuki

Sketch of a Tanforan Barracks

RITSUKO NAKAHIRA IWASA

Current Residence: Sacramento, California
Prewar Residence: Sacramento, California

Before I went to camp, we never had store-bought clothes. Everything was sewn at home. We even made rice-sack sheets. I also made some drop cloths out of rice sacks when we first came back from the camps. But after that, rice was packed in paper sacks. Before we went into camp, my mother said we couldn't afford to go out and buy new clothes. We had shopped at several dime stores like Woolworth's and Kress. So one Saturday she took us to buy underwear and things like that to take into camp.

I was one of the lucky ones in my family. They put the household things in a *kori* [woven wicker baskets with a lid which was used as luggage]. They were easy to adjust and you could pack a lot in them. I don't how I rated, but I got a suitcase! I think maybe my sister had one, too, but I don't know if the boys had them or not. From the outside it looked like black corrugated cardboard and woven, but it was all paper. I still have it. None of the clothes survived. We must have gotten new shoes because Mom took us on a shopping trip. Remember, we bought that entire yardage. However, she wasn't going to let go of any extra money because she didn't know when we would need the money. She was a strong person. I think that's why she and my dad had so many fights.

When it was time to report for camp, we were assigned to report to Florin at the railroad station there, which was our embarkation place. From there, we were sent to Arboga near Marysville. We lived in the country, but the Sacramento town people went to Wallerga, which is in Sacramento. Six blocks were set up at Arboga, and we were in the sixth block because we were the last ones to go into that camp. We lived in regular Army barracks. They were brand new; green timber. It was built to house us Japanese. I don't think it was Camp Beale, an Army installation. I thought, "Gee, we're prisoners because there were armed soldiers on our train. I think they believed we were from Japan."

From Arboga we took a train to our permanent camp, Tule Lake. I remember the guards who were on that train. I think we spent one night on the train. We lived in Block 10, which were mostly Florin people. Amy Yamada Masaki was in my block. She was the only one from Sacramento. My neighbors from Arboga were in the same block, too.

We went to school there. I didn't work at all in Tule. There were some Washington people in our camp and they were in a different section. We had some resident teachers who were former college grads or students. I remember one who taught typing. There were very few typewriters so we had to use paper keyboards and you had to learn from that. There were some typewriters, but there just weren't enough of them to go around. The smart ones knew how to get them but, you know, us farm kids were a little slow. We weren't aggressive enough to get first in line.

I took bookkeeping from a Miss Jinguji. She was from Washington State. I took algebra and geometry. I took Latin, too. A local Riverside (an area in Sacramento) boy taught geometry. I think his name was Bill Ishimoto and he was a college student. The kids from Riverside who knew him got away with murder. I didn't know him, but the others were active, but eventually the class calmed down. Things were more disciplined and organized. Tule Lake was peaceful in those days. For a while some kids would act up or show off how smart they were, but after a bit they quieted down. I spent my sophomore year in Tule.

During the Segregation Period, the majority of our family did not want to pledge allegiance to Japan and my brother did not want to go to Japan, so that's the concession my parents made to remain in this country. Satoru Joe was loyal to the United States but he was not going to serve in the Army. I think Joe signed up as "Yes-No," but I am not sure, when they changed the loyalty questionnaire. But he said he was not going to join the Army. So we went to Topaz on the rickety trains.

About attending school in Topaz: You know, if you're a country kid you always feel like a country kid and you always feel different. I have a big inferiority complex: *inaka mono yo* [country bumpkin]. When we were in Tule, I guess it was because the people from Washington were more sophisticated compared to farmers who came from Florin and Riverside, the farm country. Those people dressed much better and seemed worldlier. And in Topaz, the San Francisco people were definitely more sophisticated than us country people. Even though I lived away from my childhood friends, you still look for and feel more comfortable with people with the farm background.

What I remember about Topaz High are the teachers: One was a Kiyo Katayama (she married a Tanaka from Sacramento) and she taught shorthand, and Bob Maggiora taught bookkeeping and he was an okay teacher. I took beginning bookkeeping at Tule Lake and he taught advanced. He later became financial officer for Santa Rosa. We used to tease him about him and Miss Matzkin, who he was dating. Miss Matzkin taught sex education class and she was naming the parts of the female genital organs and she explained: there was a *minora* and a *majora* and they were different lobes of the vulva, and the kids caught on and just laughed. She was very smart. I'm not quite sure of the spelling, but look it up and see if I am right. I think I had a Mr. Westover for one of my classes. Remember Motoichi Yanagi? I think he graduated Topaz High in the first class. Well, he tried to teach us Japanese after school, but I didn't get very far.

In Topaz, I remember Miss Hosoi. She taught algebra II and one other class. We used to take advanced algebra in what is normally used in the other blocks as the laundry room. I don't remember when we moved to the regular barracks. I don't think there were even ten women in that class. I think one of them was Kumi Ishida. The boys used to give Miss Hosoi such a bad time. Sambo led the group to see how much they could embarrass her. In this same class they would try to make up some algebraic formula, using their initials, to tease Miss Hosoi about her boyfriend Hiro Katayama. Junji Doami, our senior class president, was in the class, too. She really tried to control this class. Rosie Kumekawa used to tease her, too. Miss Hosoi threatened that she would seat each rowdy boy next to a girl;

K. Kido photo

Guardtower

so we girls had to pay the price. I think I got Sam Nakaso.

My brother decided to resist the draft. There were four others from Topaz: The three Yoshida brothers and this other guy. My brother's friend said he was changing his mind and he was going into the service. He said he was leaving that night, so I said, "Good luck," and he went into the service. I really got it from the younger sister of that guy. He came back into camp but the family wouldn't let him in the barracks and they would not talk to him. It was kind of sad for everybody. Here we were, it's Christmas time and we are caroling in the snow; the snow was falling in this dark night, the moon was high, and the watchtower with a guard was silhouetted in the background. And I thought this one difficult decision had to be made by many people as to whether they should serve or not serve in the Army while they and their families were held behind barbed wire in a concentration camp.

It was the Tule Lake group that started the resisting. My brother did go for his Army physical but did not report for induction in Salt Lake City. His reason was that he was already a prisoner of war, so why should he go to another prison? Joe always said he would do things his own way and it was nobody's business because everybody had to do things their own way.

It was a few months after my brother graduated high school, so maybe it was in the fall of 1944, when the authorities came to our room to pick up my brother in the middle of the night. I heard that they had gone to the movie house [in the rec hall] and asked if my brother was in there, but they didn't give any reason. I don't know if they were military people because they had on civilian clothes. He had time to pack his things; they handcuffed him and he was gone.

He was taken to the sheriff's office in Salt Lake City. There were about half a dozen resisters from Topaz. The sheriff said these *Nisei* were no threat and took them out of their cells and put them in a basement room where they were able to do their own cooking. They were not free; they were still confined to quarters.

My mother and I went to Salt Lake City in late November to attend Joe's trial. That was when we met the mother of the three Yoshida boys who were also resisters from Topaz. Mrs. Yoshida had her eldest daughter with her and, like me, she had to accompany the mother to act as translator and interpreter.

Joe was sent to a federal penitentiary in Tucson, Arizona, and later transferred to Latoona, Texas federal prison. President Truman issued clemency orders [carries weight of erasing crime] to release the *Nikkei* resisters before Christmas of 1947 or 1948.

Joe wrote home about once a week. He worked in the laundry while in prison. He often wrote that, "So-and-so went over the hill," and that he wished he could go, too, which was not a cool thing to write because all mail was censored. The folks used to send Joe packages during the holidays. Maybe they sent him clothing, too, because when he returned he wore civilian clothes. Most people did not know he was a draft resister.

TERUKO KANEKO

Current Residence: Atherton, California
Prewar Residence: Menlo Park, California

My father was born in Hiroshima, Japan, and he came over when he was sixteen years old. My mother was born in Watsonville and so she's a *Nisei*. She was born in 1906, the year of the big earthquake in San Francisco. My mother raised five children and so she was at home most of the time. She was doing dressmaking, like making silk pajamas for the Indian store and other people. She was working for the wives of some of the Stanford professors doing dressmaking for them. And my father was a landscape gardener. When he first came from Japan, he was like a jack-of-all-trades.

The curfew affected us because my father's *Issei*, right? So he couldn't travel outside of five miles. And my grandparents lived in Gilroy at that time. I remember my mother driving the five of us over there and we had a flat tire. My mother had never gone that far without my father. My brothers were too little to change it. But fortunately we were near a friend's place and we asked them to take care of the flat tire, so we got it fixed. It was really sad my father couldn't go. My father wasn't arrested. He was active in church and the Nichi Bei Kyo Kai, too. So we were afraid, because so many of his friends were taken in. But fortunately he wasn't.

I guess my mother talked to our Stanford friends and they said they would take care of our place and so we didn't have to sell anything, fortunately. But I know my mother had to pack things away to have the house ready for rental. Then we could only bring two things and my mother took her sewing machine, fortunately. And so for these three and a half years she made clothing for us and for our friends and it really kept her busy. We did order a lot of things, but through the mail order she bought a lot of yardage so she could sew.

We got to Tanforan by bus. I think they took us up to San Mateo to the high school. I don't remember. I'd never been to a racetrack. To me it was huge! We had to live in the horse stalls. We lived on the opposite side from the grandstand. I remember we had to change the straw in the mattress. But we were very fortunate. My father's best friend was a cook for Mrs. Starr Jordan. Her husband was the first president of Stanford University. He was gone by the time I knew them. Every Sunday she would get her chauffeur to drive her to Tanforan. She brought us the comic section of the *Chronicle* and she would bring us candy and cookies, ice cream every single Sunday. She was so sweet. Oh, yes, I remember the food: chocolate pudding and liver. Fortunately, we all liked liver and so that part was okay.

I attended art school. I really enjoyed that part of it aside from the high school. I just remember one high school teacher, Mr. Bando. I think he was a math teacher. I think he was the only teacher I remember. He must have really impressed us. What I enjoyed was the talent shows. Do

Tanforan Horse Stables Apartments

you remember Goro Suzuki? I did like that and I remember the songs from that time. Those were the fun times.

Topaz: It was bleak. I never saw a sight like that. For me, the weather was bad. After my first surgery, I was paralyzed the first time because I had a cyst inside my spinal cord. And when they tried to remove it, they were worried and they removed only part of it because they were afraid that if they went in deeper it would sever all my nerves. Gradually, I was able to walk again. But in the wintertime after the snow—you know how everything melts and it's all muddy? When I was walking along, all the mud clung to the sole of my boots and I remember I was having a hard time, and my legs were weak. So that's what bothered me. I don't know if it bothered other people. I had my back surgery when I was sixteen. When I was fifteen and I went to work as a nurse's aide, that's when the doctors noticed it. So after that they sent me to the Latter Day Saints Hospital in Salt Lake City. I can't remember how long I was there, but my mother had to come with me. She stayed with me in a hotel. I guess Dr. [James] Goto and Dr. [John] Teshima both noticed that I was limping.

I remember very little of my training as a nurse's aide. But I must have been taught how to take temperature and pulse and blood pressure and things like that. But I didn't really work that long. Maybe one or two months? But I liked it. And the rest of my life I spent so much time in the hospital it's like a second home to me.

When I came back from the hospital in Salt Lake, I had to stay in the hospital in Topaz for a long time. I know aides were given a lot of responsibilities that shouldn't have been given to them. But, no choice; they didn't have enough nurses. But it was a good learning experience.

I just remember just a few of the teachers: A Mrs. Mary MacMillan. And I took Spanish from a Miss Sugihara. There was the math teacher, Asa Fujie. There was Barbara Loomis, who was short and had crutches. She was very nice, but I can't remember what she taught. And I remember Miss Gerard and Mr. Ostlund. I remember he was hard of hearing. I know there were some outstanding teachers, but on the whole I guess they were retired or not the best teachers. That's why I can't believe how many of us went to college.

To me, the reparations money was too little too late. If it had happened while my parents were alive, it would have meant a lot for them. They sacrificed so much for us. To me, it really didn't mean anything. They were the ones who really needed it. I hate to say that. We were young and it didn't bother us so much. It's my parents. I'm sure it really bothered them.

JOE YOSHIMITSU KIMURA

Current Residence: Cardiff-By-The-Sea, California
Prewar Residence: San Francisco, California

I was born in San Francisco on February 14, 1927. My parents both came from Tottori-ken, Japan in 1918. They were married in San Francisco. My dad had a variety of jobs including commercial fishing. My mother worked as a domestic.

I was the only child in my family. I was attending Roosevelt Junior High School when World War II broke out. Just prior to being evacuated to Tanforan Assembly Center in San Bruno, my father sold his car and withdrew all the monies from his bank account (what little we had) My classmates were shocked that we were being evacuated. My teacher sent me a class picture when I was in Tanforan. In Tanforan, we lived in the infield barracks and did not have to live in horse stables as others did.

The train ride to Topaz was exciting. We knew the waiters in the dining car. They were from San Francisco. I thought the meals in the dining car were beautiful. It was my first experience eating in a dining car. The first thing I remembered about Topaz was the powdery dust. All the dust storms, barrenness, and the barbed wire made it more desolate than Tanforan. Coming from beautiful San Francisco to the desert was a big shock. We came from nice-and-cool to very hot.

The barracks, the facilities, the people, the mess hall were better than Tanforan. I thought attending high school in Topaz was fun. I didn't study much, but I enjoyed all my friends and football. Being on the high school football team gave me an opportunity to leave camp and visit nearby outside schools. I went out of camp to do seasonal work with some of my friends. I wasn't the best picker or worker, but it was fun getting out of camp. In retrospect, fooling around and having fun with friends were we teenagers' means of coping with the incarceration. Since I had no siblings, I became very close to my camp friends. Richard "Ratcho" Yamashiro lived across the barracks from me. Clem Nakai and Harumi Kojimoto lived in Block 6.

After high school graduation, I went to Detroit, Michigan, knowing I would soon be drafted. I worked at an electroplating factory. Then I received a draft notice back at Topaz. I was in the Army for two years and the war ended while I was taking basic training, so I never went overseas. After being discharged, I returned to San Francisco and attended junior college for a year. Then I went to an airplane mechanics school. I also worked the post office. During this time I met Tamie Tayama, who was attending San Francisco State University. We fell in love and got married in 1953. After our marriage, my wife and I moved to Los Angeles. I worked at the flower market and purchased a share of the grounds and nursery of the Tayama Greenhouse in Encinitas, California. I am still working there on a part-time basis, but my son and two sons-in-law have taken over the total operation and I work as a flunky to them.

Retirement activities include some work, travel, and sometimes fishing. I've never missed a class reunion or a

Topaz reunion! My general health is borderline everything, but [I] get around pretty well for my age. I've had all kinds of knee surgeries. My mother died of cancer, but my dad lived to the ripe old age of ninety-three!

I enjoy meeting with my old Topaz friends and have kept most of my high school relationships alive with reunions and visits. I also traveled with some of my classmates. We keep our Topaz relationships active, since both my wife and I have no siblings. We value these camp friendships.

We did not want the redress funds. But since our parents were not alive to get any of it, we accepted the money and try to remember them with donations to various Japanese American organizations and charitable causes. We were young enough just to go and be interned, but later we understood why older people were unwilling. We are concerned that this never happens again to our children or anyone else. We have discussed the incarceration with our children, but we could not do this when we were younger. Obviously, we felt ashamed in some way and our parents did not talk about it either. Now my wife goes to the high schools and community college classes to share her experiences. She has been interviewed numerous times to tell her story.

JUNE SAKIKO EGASHIRA KOBA

Current Residence: Monterey Park, California
Prewar Residence: Centerville, California

My folks were devastated by the ordeal. Our family was first evacuated to Tanforan Race Track in San Bruno, California. Since there were seven in our family, we were assigned to the centerfield barracks. Some families had to sleep in the horse stables that smelled so badly you felt like vomiting from the foul manure odor.

After approximately three months, we were taken by an old vintage train, (packed like a boxcar loaded with cattle), and evacuated from California to Salt Lake City, Utah. We were then taken by bus to the desert area near Topaz Mountain, Delta, Utah. We were told to draw the shades down every time our train passed a town or city. The day I arrived at Topaz camp and seeing all the barbed-wire fence and armed military guards, I was personally frightened by the scene. Some of the barracks were missing roofs.

Our family was assigned to Apartment C-D, one room, with no privacy whatsoever. We were told to go to a certain block to stuff a canvas cover with hay, which was to be our mattress to sleep on. We used army blankets as partitions and tried to adjust to camp life and made the best of a bad situation. The military guards were at their posts to keep us from escaping. We were warned not to go beyond the gates.

At first I cried a great deal, not understanding completely or knowing that was going to happen to our family and me. There were questions such as "What was a teenager like me to do about finishing school?" "How would camp life change me personally?" I felt frustrated, angered, and quite concerned about my future.

I remember I had to haul a wheelbarrow full of black coal for the potbelly stove we used for heating in the freezing cold. It created a lot of soot. I remember using the scrub board to wash bed sheets and clothes. There were no washers or dryers then. There were no more family meals together after we got to camp. Everything was army style. My mother (Asaye Adachi) worked in the block mess hall kitchen, while my dad (Rikizo George Egashira)—after he recovered from heart attack suffered shortly after arriving at camp—worked as block fire inspector. At the beginning, I recall how often the internees would get diarrhea from the food they had to eat, and how crowded the latrines became. I couldn't imagine eating tripe, but instead, I cried. Those were the "Get out of my way, I've got the runs" days.

As years went by, things got better. I adjusted and got into the routine of going to school and working for Mr. Robert Maggiora. He was also my teacher who taught students majoring in business. He was responsible for teaching me all that I applied to my work during my postwar period. He was one of many teachers who volunteered to help the Japanese. I worked for him at the school administrative office, part-time after school during my junior and senior years. The teaching staff at Topaz High was great.

They were dedicated teachers who were committed to doing a good job under difficult times and circumstances.

The food at camp got better as the cooks learned a few lesson on how to cook by then. There were baseball games. Teams were formed between various clubs and blocks. Hobby clubs were formed. Canteen and movies were provided if you didn't mind sitting on the floor. During senior prom night, I remember dancing to the music of the best bands. Records by Dorsey, Goodman, Artie Shaw, Glenn Miller, Count Basie, and, last but not least, Harry James, were played. I fondly remember songs such as "Don't Fence Me In," "I'll Never Smile Again," "Deep in the Heart of Texas," "Chattanooga Choo Choo," "Dancing in the Dark," "In the Mood," "Sleepy Lagoon." That was great music! (My senior aerobics instructor plays these oldies during workouts.)

After the war, there was no way my dad and mom would be able to restart the family business. It is my firm belief that his illness was due to the disruption of his family-owned business and evacuation. I felt the impact of his heart attack and insecurity. Someone had to stay with mom and dad. I felt I was dealt those cards. My dad became a naturalized citizen postwar. He was very proud to get his citizenship papers. Our parents worked very hard to raise their family. They were the pioneers who paved the way for the second generation. We owe them a great deal. They truly sacrificed so much.

I have not gone back to Topaz. It is my understanding that there is nothing remaining except for a few memorial markers. I sometimes wonder how my life would have been if it were not for President Roosevelt's Executive Order 9066 that changed the direction of my life. I still feel I was cheated of my adolescence years of fun years. After "Class of '45" I really had to grow up in a hurry. I didn't even know how to cook!

Class of '45

From 1943 Ramblings Yearbook

GEORGE S. "DORSEY" KOBAYASHI

Current Residence: St. Louis, Missouri
Prewar Residence: Oakland, California

When the war broke out, I was attending Westlake Junior High School along with Bob Utsumi, Dorothy Harada, Kei Yoshiura, Shin Tanaka, Hidetoshi Takahashi, Seiko Akahoshi, and a few other Japanese Americans. While I had anxieties as to what would happen to us as a result of Pearl Harbor, the thing that bothered me most was the appearance of lapel buttons on other Asian students identifying them as Chinese Americans, Korean Americans, or Filipino Americans. Such is life and, despite this behavior, we continued to attend school with support from many of our friends and teachers.

My mother had to deal with preparing for our move to Topaz without our father, who was sent to Arroyo Del Valle Sanitarium with tuberculosis. Herded onto trains, the ride to an uncertain destination was frightening. For many of us this would be the first time we would be out of California, and, in our case, without our father. During the daylight hours it was an education to see parts of the United States that I had never seen. At night, however, we saw very little, not even house or streetlights as we passed through various cities and towns, owing to the imposed military blackouts. In general it was not a very pleasant trip since we had to sit upright during the entire trip to Topaz.

Arriving at Delta, we were put onto buses for our ride to our new quarters. The ride to Topaz was uneventful until we arrived at the barbed-wire enclosure that would be home to me for the next three years. My most memorable impression was stepping off the bus into the talc-like powdery dust that covered the ground. We were welcomed to Topaz by a drum-and-bugle group, but their music did little to cheer us up. My first impression of our new environment was that it was bleak, hot, with fine dust from the clay soil swirling around, and the environs fit only for rattlesnakes and sagebrush. Topaz was still in the process of being put together and there were several areas under construction. It was situated on a site that was one mile on each side, fenced with barbed wire, and guard towers located at each corner and half way in between.

In contrast to the school system that was hastily put together at Tanforan, the school at Topaz was better organized and provided an adequate, though limited, environment for learning. While I've heard a lot of criticism leveled at the caliber and qualification of some of the teachers that were recruited from the "outside," in general, I thought the faculty did an admirable job in providing us with an education. In addition to the counselors who were available to help us and provide some guidance, the school system was designed to give the students a limited choice in designing their curriculum according to their needs and ambitions. Attending school was one of the highlights that I looked forward to each day. I feel that I got an adequate

Topaz High School Library

education, although my classmates might beg to differ since my mischievous behavior was probably a big distraction for them.

Looking back through time, the success of Topaz High School speaks well for itself by the records of its graduates. My extracurricular activities consisted of holding one of the class offices in the student government, and acting as a teacher's aide, grading language papers in Spanish and French, and also in mathematics. My most important extracurricular activity, however, consisted of being the *itazura ko* [prankster], and living up to my senior class will and testimony, viz., willing "my ability to get away with murder to all those not so fortunate." The most memorable situation happened on the last day of school. While running around—being chased by the rest of my classmates for something I had precipitated—I was run over by a two-ton truck and broke my leg, resulting in my being laid up in traction for the entire summer of 1944.

As I look back on my days in Topaz, growing up in camp was truly an experience for me. I was short, scrawny, underweight, and not much of an athlete. My daily activities were rather mundane and consisted of such things as whiling away my time visiting the canteen, working on the pig farm, going to the library to read, hunting arrowheads in the desert, catching scorpions, participating in the Boy Scouts, and learning the rudiments of bridge and pinochle. Participating in the Boy Scouts gave me an opportunity to broaden my intellectual curiosity. Prior to evacuation, I was a member of Troop 36 that consisted of boys in the Japanese American community in Oakland. There was Bob Utsumi and Shin Tanaka (Topaz High School Class of '45), Shinji Momono and Shichiro Yokomizo (Class of '44), and several others, but our troop leader stood out heads and shoulders over all of us: Bill Oshima. I mention this because Bill was a natural leader, very prominent at Topaz High School, someone I looked up to, and a great influence on my future development.

As extroverted as I may have appeared to my classmates, I was not very socially mature. That is not to say I was not interested in girls, but in the three years I spent in high school I never dated nor did I go to any of the proms. Be that as it may, those who know me well will attest to the fact that I certainly made up the deficiency, as I grew older!

YURI OBATA KODANI

Current Residence: Oakland, California
Prewar Residence: Berkeley, California

My name is Lillian Yuri Kodani and I was born on April 14, 1927. My father came from Sendai and his name was Chiura Obata and he came here in 1903. My mother was Haruko Obata and she came from Fukuoka in 1910.

I went to the Berkeley schools until I went to camp. I went to high school near St. Louis, in Webster Groves, Missouri. We came back and my dad started teaching at UC Berkeley again and I went to Cal and got a BA and MA in fine arts. My husband graduated with an architecture degree and we married in 1949 and moved to Oakland and we have lived here ever since.

Our life before the war was very pleasant. My father always invited the professors from Cal, and his students to our home. My mother taught *ikebana*, so her students would come to the house. We lived very well and we had many friends here. My father's students and his fellow professors were very upset when we had to evacuate and leave California.

About Pearl Harbor: My brother came over that Sunday morning and he looked really upset and pale and said, "Something terrible has happened and we're at war with

Japan and I don't know what is going to happen to all of us." My parents were also upset.

The neighbors' reaction was fine. And school was okay, too. The teachers were understanding. There was one incident: A classmate's mother told me that I couldn't play with her daughter now that I was the enemy. I went home and told my parents and they said, "You mustn't think that at all. You were born here and you are a citizen and you're not the enemy."

We didn't own our home, so my mother had to sell all the plants and the furniture. The university stored all my dad's paintings at the president's house and the women's gym. My mother taught flower arrangement and so she had a lot of vases and equipment. One of her friends had a store and so she took all of the vases and stored them at her place. Then other people stored our other possessions and so we didn't miss anything. Nothing got lost.

It was so cold and rainy that day and the irony of it was that we evacuated from the First Congregational Church in Berkeley and my brother had just gotten married four or five months before in that same church. The people there were so nice. They served doughnuts and coffee. Then we got on the buses and drove across the bridge. It was sad. It was raining and everyone was weepy. Then we got to Tanforan and the barracks weren't all complete, so we had to sleep in the horse stalls. It was just whitewashed. That was it, with three army cots in each stall that the three of us had to share, one light bulb, and that was it. The door was a horse door, divided in half, top and bottom.

At the time I was really horse crazy and used to save money and go riding in the Berkeley Hills. So I was in seventh heaven. But my mother was so upset and said,

"We're treated like animals," and she started to cry. In all these years I had never seen her cry. She was very stoic. I was shocked. I said, "Why are you crying?" We were moved out of there as soon as they finished the barracks. We were put in one room. My poor brother: Newly married, with his in-laws and his parents and me in one room. Poor guy!

When we first got to Tanforan, my father immediately realized there'd be people who didn't have anything to do. They were busy working and trying to make homes for the children, and the children also were at loose ends. So he wanted to start an art school and he got permission to use one of the barracks. He went there one morning to open it to see what was in there, and two little girls were waiting in the rain for him to open. He was so pleased that people

Street Scence from the Grandstand Looking at the Barracks

were interested. He got the supplies from his fellow professors at Cal, and other students would bring paper and paint. Stores contributed also, like Flax Art Store. It was very heartwarming to see this response. He got people like my brother who went to the art department to teach classes, and other artists. Like Hisako Hibi, and her husband, Matsusaburo Hibi, Koho Yamamoto, and Hatsuro Aizawa from San Francisco. He called anyone with an art background to come and help. He had good response. Many *Issei* never had time to pursue any hobby and so they were so happy to attend. He would take kids on a sketching trip around the racetrack, where there was a park in the center of the camp.

Then we had to get ready to move to Topaz. He opened an art school immediately. He had a good connection with the head of the camp, Mr. Ernst, who wanted to help in every way, so he provided him with a barracks. He used half of the barracks and the other was used for something else. There was another artist, Mine Okubo, who went to Cal. I think she was a student of his at one time. And she helped with the camp newspaper by doing illustrations.

When people came to visit the camp, the director would always drag my father out to be the entertainment after the dinner. He would invite people from the audience to make one stroke and he would make a painting out of it. He was very quick. The *sumi-e* that he did was very, very quick. And he would let the person have the painting. An American woman came and she was a reporter or something. And she said, "I'm going to stump you." She made a red square in the middle of this paper. Then he came up and looked and looked at it and then painted a beautiful sunset behind it. In the desert we could appreciate a beautiful

sunset every night. And then at the very end he made a fence post for this red square and drew the barbed wire with a sign every twenty yards that said "All Japanese cannot go beyond this point!" And that was the sign that ruined this beautiful sunset. He just looked at her and smiled.

She was sort of shocked, but she took it with her. It was great.

They also came to camp to ask for a painting to present to Mrs. Eleanor Roosevelt, wife of US president Franklin D. Roosevelt, because she tried to help as much as she could. So he made a nice painting of camp showing the barracks by moonlight. And they presented it to her. We found out later that it's in her home at Warm Springs, Georgia. The director said any time we visit we were welcome to come to see the painting. It's very nice to know that it's appreciated.

In school we had mostly *Nisei* teachers until later. We had volunteer friends come in and help out. I just remember the *Nisei* teachers. They were very good. The students that I went to Willard Junior High with in Berkeley came with us: Mary Matsumoto, Mary Fukada, and also Aileen Yamate of San Francisco. It was good to go to school to get your mind off of where we were. At that time I wasn't interested in anything particular, so I took a general course. It was okay. I took art classes with my dad at his school. That was fine.

I attended Topaz High for only half a year because our family had to leave camp for safety reasons. Young men had to sign-up for the "No-No," "Yes-Yes" business (the loyalty questions). There were meetings every night and my father and brother tried to counsel the young men to sign up for the Army so that it would prove that we are all loyal, and we would get out of camp sooner. But one of the *Kibei* men who disagreed with him was waiting for him when he came out of the central shower to walk back to our barracks. He tried to hit him real hard on the head but my father put his arm up to lessen the blow. He was hit across the temple and stumbled down, but he grabbed some gravel and threw it at the man's face and blinded him. My father has a very big voice and he yelled very loud and the man ran away. He was bleeding from a scalp wound and he ran to our barracks and yelled through the door that he'd been attacked. He told us to "lock the door and don't open it!—I'm going to the hospital." It was about five blocks away from our barracks. He walked to the hospital and they patched him up. My mother went the next day to pick up this Japanese padded robe he wore after his bath. She brought it back and there was blood all down one side of it. Somehow the muscle connected to the eye was not operable at the hospital because there was no eye surgeon there. It was safer to leave. We could go to Salt Lake City and get treatment there.

We had friends who ran the *Pacific Citizen* newspaper [official organ of the National Japanese American Citizens League], Larry Tajiri and Tsuguyo Okagaki Tajiri. We stayed with them. Tsuguyo's parents lived in San Jose and my father was an old, old, friend of theirs, so it was easy to get there. It was the first time out of camp and it was wonderful—to eat hamburgers and to see trees!

I thought the reparations and compensation were long overdue. When it came it was enough, but people didn't know what to do with it. We donated most of it back to causes we thought were important. My brother and my dad passed away and so they weren't able to get it, but my mother, my husband, and I were able to get it.

SACHIKO KINOSHITA KUME

Current Residence: Atherton, California
Prewar Residence: Oakland, California

Tomoye Katayama and I were at a Buddhist church in Oakland on December 7th and we decided to take in a movie instead of having a party at the church. They stopped the movie and announced that all Navy personnel had to report to the Naval station. I didn't know what was going on. As we got out of the movie house, I see all the newspapers that said "Extra, extra!! Pearl Harbor bombed!!"

At Topaz I was in Block 12-4-B. We were six of us in the family and we had just the one room, second to the end. Next door was a couple who were pharmacists. They had a pharmacy in San Jose. Next door to us was the Kawakami family. They had a big family, so they occupied two rooms. There was a potbelly stove and that's it. My dad made partitions to separate the kitchen and the bedroom. I don't know where he got the wood, but we had cloth and we just draped it over each partition to make it homey.

I worked part-time as a nurse's aide. My friend and I were the first group to try and get a job, so we just asked if we could do some work. This was Takeko Kawakami, her older sister May Kawakami, Emma Matsumoto, and I.

The nurse offered a class for us. I can't remember how many days we went to class, but she taught us all the basics. Pediatrics was my favorite. From there I went to obstetrics. I must have been around sixteen.

I used to hike up to Topaz Mountain with three sisters, Takeko, Umeko, and Lily Kawakami. We used to look for topaz stones. There were stones all over, encrusted in the rocks. It was walking distance. You have to actually have some sort of tools, for they're all in the rocks, but I was able to dig out one topaz stone. We used to look for arrowheads out in the desert. I found a lot of arrowheads. There were a lot of seashells, too. There must have been a sea once. My dad made seashell jewelry. I still have that corsage that he made out of seashells. I still have that.

K. Kido photo

Drum and Bugle Welcoming Band, Topaz

RYOZO GLENN KUMEKAWA

Current Residence: Wakefield, Rhode Island
Prewar Residence: San Francisco, California

My parents were prohibited by racist laws from becoming naturalized US citizens. Despite a half a century of work in America, the fruits of their labor went down the tube in a couple of weeks after the announcement of the evacuation. The pain and trauma caused by evacuation resulted in my mother to get physically ill at both Tanforan and at Topaz. I can still see her sitting on that metal cot, hand clenched together, in that horse stable at Tanforan. Despite her despair, like any mother, she made sure that we all had bedrolls and what-have-you. She was the one who organized everything and made sure that what we carried into camp was usable. She took it all and developed ulcers under all the stress.

We spent about half a year at Tanforan. We were in horse stalls. Our immediate reaction was to put up some sheets to provide some personal privacy for my sister and for my parents.

I recall there was a lot of mud around and that we organized our school. I remember that Henry Tani, the only graduate student in education, was asked to be the principal of the high school. All the teachers were college students. They were all pursuing professional or job-oriented majors. None of them were majors in languages or music or history; they were all occupation-oriented. I remember having classes in anatomy and subjects of this kind. This was an informal school system that was established and taught by internees themselves.

At the end of 1942, in October, we were taken by train to Delta, Utah. Because of the war, there was huge demand for all rolling stock. So they took these Pullman cars out of mothballs. You could tell because if you poked the seats with your finger, a cloud of dust would rise. The cars had pull-down beds. There were sentries at the front and back of each coach. They had steel helmets and bayoneted guns. My God, and then here are these Black stewards treating us as if we were first-class passengers on the train. The stewards behaved as if this were a normal day at work. The contrast was just stunning.

We organized a student-activities discussion. One was titled, "Are We Americans?" It was an open session for students who wanted to participate in this sort of discussion. This took place in the context of school, but without teacher supervision. The teachers probably knew what was going on because we put up enough signs everywhere. We had about ten to fifteen students participating. I'm not sure if we ever came to an agreement or a consensus. It was simply that we were addressing the issue. We simply asked, "Under the circumstances, are we Americans?" It's very strange, because I was not an American citizen, but all the way through I just denied my Japanese national citizenship. I just totally identified with the fact that, like my brothers and sisters and friends, I was an American citizen. I was naturalized as soon as the McCarran Act was passed in 1952.

We were trying to replicate inside the camp what we understood to be the typical high-school conditions outside as we perceived them in the lives of our older brothers and sisters. Whether it had to do with dances or organizations, they derived from experiences we heard from older brothers and sisters. One of the biggest thrills was to wear my older brother's Lowell High School letterman's sweater. The kinds of organizations we had in camp was a play-out of what we heard from older brothers and sisters.

We didn't acknowledge the impact of the Japanese American evacuee teachers as much as we did, for example, Muriel Mazkins, who later became the wife of the governor of Pennsylvania. But we didn't give that kind of recognition to the evacuee teachers, although they provided us with both attention and guidance. The reason for this is that the non–Japanese American teachers we admired and respected represented what we idealistically believed was the best of the world that we felt abandoned us. We did not fully acknowledge the contributions of internee teachers like Eiko Hosoi.

I was scared when I left the camp. I was totally afraid to get out of camp into an alien world of which I knew so little. Topaz still provided a known and safe haven; a port in the face of a storm, even with all the insidious implications of the racist removal from our homes in the Bay Area.

KIYOSHI JIM KUSUNOKI

Current Residence: Minneapolis, Minnesota

Prewar Residence: San Francisco, California

Our prewar address was 1375 Pine Street. It was on the corner of Pine and Larkin Streets. I went to the Redding Elementary School. There was a Methodist Church next door. I was a loner there. I had more *hakujin* friends. The Pine Methodist Church was a Japanese church. I had a few friends there, but we went our separate ways. My father was a tailor. He lost his business and the property that he had stored. He also gave away a lot of property to a Chinese friend who was in the same type of business.

We were sent to the Tanforan Assembly Center. We lived in the barracks and not in the horse stables. My high school days are sort of zero. I played a little basketball and I just took classes that I had to: English, history. I spent most of my senior year in Ann Arbor, Michigan. Andy (Handa) and Mas (Nonaka) went to high school there. I had enough credits so I ended up coming back to Topaz because I received my draft notice. That's why I graduated with the class of '45. Actually, I screwed up. I should have stayed to finish up my senior year in camp. It would have been my best year and I could have played a lot of basketball. One of the reasons I went out was I thought I could play ball. I could have made the team, but I had to be a resident, so I couldn't play anyway.

My father taught tailoring at Topaz. Many classmates took his tailoring class. I can't remember a whole lot. The only time I went on a date was the senior prom. For the life of me, I can't remember who I took. I remember getting a corsage and a box of candy, but I can't remember who the girl was. Isn't that sad? I don't have any yearbooks to go back to look through because my yearbooks never made it out of camp. I left Topaz before my folks did and then I went into the service. I spent all of 1946 in Germany with the 60th Infantry Occupational Forces. When I got out of the service, they were already out of camp and resettled in Chicago and many of my things were gone.

In retirement, I am involved in volunteer work. I run the machine that produces the monthly newsletter for our church. I also deliver "Meals on Wheels" through our church to deliver meals to shut-ins. I see Andy once in a while. He is the only contact with the people from camp. The reparations money was way too late for my parents.

K. Kido photo

Panoramic View of Topaz Camp

RURIKO MARUBAYASHI LEE

Current Residence: Alameda, California
Prewar Residence: Alameda, California

My father Bunju Marubayashi came to America as a teenager to join his father, Seisaku Marubayashi. He farmed in different areas and later did gardening and also cooked for a White family in the evenings. My mother did "day work," which was cleaning the homes of rich White families. Most *Issei* wives in Alameda did day work and men did gardening.

My mother passed away at age forty-one in May of 1943 while she was in a sanitarium for tuberculosis. We were living in Topaz. My father was not allowed to go back to California when my mother died and there was no funeral for her. The hospital had my mother cremated and her ashes were sent to us in Topaz.

I completed my high school education at Topaz High and graduated in June of 1945. The school system and curriculum were quite lax. Some of the teachers were okay. The others must have just graduated from teachers' colleges and Topaz must have been their first teaching assignment.

I really enjoyed the tailoring class taught by Mr. Kusunoki. We learned how to make shirts and learned how to draft patterns. I made myself some shirts. We got some GI clothing and the rest we ordered from the mail-order catalogs. I didn't join any groups or clubs at Topaz. I just went to school. I took basic courses like algebra, English, science. I had boyfriends. I had a lot of pen pals in Canada, like a gal who was in a camp up there. Also some people in other camps. But I never got to meet any of them. I used to write to a few soldiers during wartime, but I lost track of everybody.

I did try to keep in touch with other people after I left camp. My grandson in Hawaii had a project in school and he wanted to know about camp life and he wrote a paper about that. Now, his father, my second son, has become very interested in my camp experience and he wants more information. His son is going to the Air Force Academy and after visiting him there, he decided to stop by to visit Manzanar on his way back home via California. He looked over the campsite and could not believe the conditions under which we all lived behind barbed wire during World War II. Now, anytime there is a PBS special on the camp experience, he makes sure to watch it. My other children and grandchildren have not shown much interest in my camp experience.

I am not angry about the incarceration experience because I was able to meet different people who are still friends. I was too young to have this experience hit me as something bad.

JEAN SANFORD LUNDSTEDT

Current Residence: Columbus, Ohio
Prewar Residence: Chicago, Illinois

At Topaz, my father, Raymond Prior Sanford, was Assistant Project Director responsible for the Community Management Program. He had asked that his family live in a barracks with the evacuees, but the authorities refused. He didn't feel we were entitled to any better housing than the evacuees. That tells a little something about his attitude.

I didn't work any place in camp. I took piano lessons with Aiko (I don't remember her last name) and I was in a recital with all these little children. I belonged to the Music Club, was news editor for the paper, and was in the Thespian Club. I remember playing *gomuko* with my father. That's a five-in-a-row Japanese game, the Japanese game *Go*.

I remember doing things with my family. We would go out on the desert and my brother loved to collect arrowheads. The kids were really mean to my brothers. They were younger and you know how older kids can be really mean sometimes. My brothers ended up going to school in Delta. There were a number of staff children who went to school in Delta.

I ran around with Kiko Nakagiri, Ellen Shimada, Fumi Saiki, and Mary Iwaki. She was valedictorian. My general impression is that the kids were smart, good socially, and more well-rounded than my friends in Chicago had been. I guess this is one of the examples of a minority having to try harder.

I admired Barbara Loomis. She was a wonderful woman. I think of her whenever I think of the desert and how she dragged those heavy braces around. Shirvey Sharvey was kind of wild and excitable. Muriel Matzkin went with Bob Maggiora. Jack Gooding had a very florid face and black hair. I remember Dave Tatsuno assigning a poem, "Give Them the Flowers Now," which has stuck with me all these years.

My father was going through a conflict with the administration. My mother said he tried to keep it from us. He didn't want us worried. But he would spend a lot of nights working at the office and I'm sure that colored my experience. Among other things, he refused to go along with the black marketing going on in camp. He also was critical of "camp" gas being used for recreation by some members of the staff.

Mr. [Matsusaburo] Hibi did a painting of my father, a very severe-looking portrait. He was one of the people who wanted to go on strike. He was very honest with my father. When my father complained that the painting made him appear severe, Mr. Hibi said, "This is what I see in you." But he was very much in favor of my father. Mr. Hibi, as the former director of Topaz Art School, wrote a letter of support for my father after he was fired for having received an "Unsatisfactory Efficiency Rating."

It's hard for me to think about this without getting angry. The injustice of it. As I think about the situation in our country today, where people are being held. It's sort of *déjà vu* and it's really scary. I feel like yelling, "This is a democracy!" I think our civil liberties are really threatened. I have always been aware of that.

I think that I have guilt. I think I have guilt because here all of my schoolmates had been evacuated. I had been evacuated, too, from Chicago, but it wasn't the same thing.

From Kazuko Hashiguchi Iwasaki

Dance Bids

KAZU "ROY" MARUOKA

Current Residence: Sonoma, California
Prewar Residence: San Francisco, California

Our neighborhood was west of today's Japantown in San Francisco. The neighborhood was ethnically integrated. Although these were the years of the Depression, it was a time when I was happily secure. I had wonderful memories of my early childhood. Such was not the case from the age of thirteen to seventeen because I spent those years incarcerated at Tanforan Race Track Assembly Center and Topaz, Utah.

The Monday after the December 7 attack on Pearl Harbor, I returned from Roosevelt Junior High and called out "*tadaima*" [I'm home] to my mother. Her greeting was not the same as usual. She said that two men came during the day. They searched my father's home office and took him away. I did not know or understand who the men were or where they had taken my father. I do not recall any sign of anger amongst us, just quiet puzzlement and sadness.

After preparing for evacuation, our family went to Kinmon Gakuen Japanese Language School on Bush and Buchanan and boarded a bus for Tanforan. As a teen, I dreaded the loss of privacy there. I had socialization problems. I was introverted, insecure, and had low self-esteem.

Photo: Kumi Ishida

*Plaque at Tanforan Shopping Center, San Bruno, Calif.
(formerly Tanforan Assembly Center)*

I had a severe eczema problem and was once even sent home from school because my face was so ugly. Because of these "wonderful" aspects of my personality, I suffered in having to live in a communal environment.

During our stay in Tanforan, we received a letter from our father. It was dated June 20, 1942, and was the first communication we had with him since he was arrested on December 8, 1941. He had been taken to Sharp Park Detention Center, but we lost track of his whereabouts. We found out that he was being held at Internment Center K-1-1914, Camp Livingston, Louisiana. My father's English was not perfect, but he wrote:

"And Kazu made me proud that you are going to school and study, try to select the subject and prepare for the college. You all must be patient and be strong be very careful your moral and body...."

Along the trail from detention camp to detention camp, my father suffered a stroke. After he arrived at Topaz so that mother could provide assistance, he was not the same man we last saw in San Francisco the day before he was taken away. Yes, it was a happy occasion for mother and father to be reunited, but it was heartbreaking to see him walking very slowly toward us with the use of a cane.

I was one of a class of thirty-one students whose entire high school years were spent in incarceration. In anticipating the closure of the camp, the administrators at Topaz High accelerated the first semester seniors to join the "real" senior class. This "deprived" me of a half-year of high school, but it was of little importance to me. I had not had a brilliant high school career anyway, through no fault of the teachers. My downfall was probably due to a lack of motivation, the absence of educational and career planning, and truly bad timing. So early graduation was my chance for a fresh start. I felt that I let my father down as I recalled his words: "...you are going to school and study, try to select the subject and prepare for the college."

At Topaz High, students carried on with academics, sports, student government, and extracurricular activities. Despite the absence of normal school facilities, we made the best of existing circumstances. We took core curriculum courses like English, social science, geometry, and electives like agricultural science and welding. During my days at Roosevelt Junior High I had played the clarinet. At Topaz, the only instrument available on loan was a trumpet and I began playing it. Each block had a recreation hall. The recreation hall in Block 42 was partly devoted to Boy Scout activities. The leader was Ichiro Sasaki. Ich was

Photo by K. Kido

Race between the Sage Brush

from Berkeley and was a drummer and a drum major. He also played the guitar. Ich organized ensembles for us to play in and we later performed at assemblies and school dances.

I remember a social science class not for its fascinating subject matter, but for the teacher, Miss Long. She was a fascinating subject, a feast for our eyes. She left Topaz for Hawaii to get married. Academic pursuits were not foremost in my Topaz-teen mind.

If there *is* a positive aspect of going to high school while incarcerated, I noticed from my perspective on the fringe that students could be popular in a number of categories. The studious one, the skilled athletes, the jokesters, the jitterbug couples, the hip ("cool" later), the student-body leaders, and those who studied diligently in preparation for subsequent education.

I consider myself a survivor because I had the opportunity to get back on track and resume my education after returning to San Francisco. The period of incarceration was an unequivocal setback for my education. Attending San Francisco State College (being a "schoolboy" notwithstanding) provided me a chance to develop and explore goals and aspirations. I was able to make up for lost time, to bolster and strengthen aspects of self-worth, and self-esteem—to become an employable individual.

SACHI KAWAHARA MASAOKA

Current Residence: San Mateo, California
Prewar Residence: San Leandro, California

You know the Executive Order? I remember one experience very vividly. The orders were posted on telephone poles. And I remember reading one when a group of kids came by. I think it was a boy's voice said, "Read it good, Jap!" while I was reading it. I said to myself, "He's not even grammatical. It should be, 'Read it well.'" I'm a grammarian to this day. If I hadn't been a kindergarten teacher, I would have been a high school English teacher.

One thing I remember about getting ready to go to camp is my parents had bought me a new blue bike—a royal blue bike—and it had balloon tires. That was my pride and joy. Having to leave that was a big sorrow. I just felt really deprived. Especially, I think, that was my first brand-new bike. I remember that I just loved that bike.

I was a good student in school. That's why I liked school. It's a place to get recognition. I think a lot of schoolteachers are good in school. That's why we associate very happy memories with classrooms. I think I worked on the yearbook. I remember we were sophomores then. I remember looking it up. I was a word lover even then, because I remember looking up the word. It comes from sophos, I think, and mors, and it means "wise fool": a paradox. I was quite interested in that. I've always been interested in origins of words; root words.

I didn't get attached to any teacher. Not one. I remember a Mrs. Nail. I mean she was really homely. She had straight gray hair, but her name is what made an impression on me. I remember Eleanor Sekerak. She was Eleanor Gerard then. But I don't remember her in relationship to me because I think she mostly taught the older kids. But I do remember her interaction with Billy Oshima. I think he had a good relationship with her, and he was like a personality-plus guy. He used to tease her about Mr. Sekerak because they were courting about that time. And she got a kick out of it. I remember the banter between the two of them.

I worked in the dental clinic. My job was to be the aide to the aide. Very prestigious! [joke] But it was fun. I remember mixing amalgam. It was for the filling. The silver filling. It was a very lowly job. One of our jobs was to ask when it was somebody's appointment time, then go out to the hall to announce their name. That made me feel like a big shot [joke]. I think we might have worn a white jacket. Were we volunteers or were we paid? I don't remember that part too well.

I don't remember movies, but I remember Morning Watch. It was a Christian prayer group. It wasn't at school. It was held in one of the mess halls in the boonies, or it might have been a rec hall. We used it early in the morning, around 6:30. It must have been before school started. I'm not sure of the sequence of events, but I do remember going to that. One of the leaders was Mary Mac, I mean Mary MacMillan. We called her Mary Mac. Bill Muramoto was one of the leaders. He was older, much older. I think he relocated to Sacramento.

I was in the Girl Reserves. I remember we made a pie. It was the best pie. We made a pie with graham-cracker crust. We crumbled it and must have added some margarine. That sort of acted like an adhesive and we patted it in this pie plate. Then we made chocolate pudding and poured the pudding into the pie crust. This was a Girl Reserve project and to me it was the best pie! Because I love chocolate. It was so yummy. I thought it was the best treat.

Rear: Marty Oshima. Front: Sachi Kawahara, Tomi Kasai, Eiko Otagiri, Unidentified

Picnic in Mountains Outside of Topaz (1943)

The internment was a terrible travesty. Our constitutional rights were deprived with no due process of the law. When I was thirteen I had no idea at all. The realization of the injustice happened gradually. I was happy to get the reparations check. I remember Tad and I each got a Toyota.

I think my peers had the greatest impact on my life in camp. It was a peer society. As adolescents, our peers had more influence than our parents. In camp I think our parents were impotent in terms of controlling our lives.

KUMIKO KARIYA MATSUMOTO

Current Residence: Castro Valley, California
Prewar Residence: East Palo Alto, California

A t Topaz, the winter, it was quite cold. I remember the fellas building a skating rink with a dirt bank. They opened up the fire hydrant and let the water flow in there and let the ice freeze. I remember one of my brothers sent through a catalog for a pair of skates for me. I thought that it was so nice of him and we had fun on that ice rink. Others would come and watch. That was our in block: Block 30, Barracks 9, Room E. There were some fun things. It wasn't all drab and miserable. Sets Yamane and Teru Tamura and I hung out together all the time. We always went for walks or sat at one or the other's home just to talk. I was glad to have such good friends. That was one of the nice things that came out of being in camp.

I went to some of the school dances. And I can remember my first date. We used to go as a group with the girls, but the first date I had was Paul Bell. And Sachi Kawahara told me later Paul was asking who he could take out and she said, "Well, Kumi's one of the tallest ones I know." So he said, "Okay." But we had a great time. I remember assemblies, but not too much of it. But I do remember I really enjoyed watching Seiko Akahoshi and Wacky Sumimoto jitterbugging. I think everybody enjoyed that. Another one was Elsie Itashiki and her singing. That stays with me.

Someone once asked me about the reparations money. This Black fellow that I worked with at Lucky Stores in one of their offices said, "Are you going to pick up your acre and your mule?" I said, "Well, if they give it to me, yes. But I'm not going to go out to fight for it." That was my feeling. When it came, yes, of course, I accepted it. I don't think too much about that. You know, if it came, it came. If they couldn't give it to us we would manage.

I hope it never happens again. And it shouldn't have happened. But I guess because it was in the days when the event happened, they were afraid. And I don't think the Japanese American community had the strong leadership that it does now. Things would have been quite different.

School Dance

PETER MATSUMOTO

Current Residence: Glencoe, Illinois
Prewar Residence: San Francisco, California

My father, Ben Toyomatsu, and mother, Teruko Matsumoto, settled in San Francisco, where they had a dry-cleaning business. There was a neighborhood family who felt terrible about the evacuation. On the day we were about to leave for camp, one of the sons rushed into the house, laid some bills in my mother's hand, and ran out with tears in his eyes.

We were first sent to the Santa Anita Race Track Assembly Center in Southern California. Most of the people from San Francisco were sent to Tanforan Race Track in San Bruno. Later, we were transferred to Topaz, Utah. I rejoined my friends from San Francisco there.

I attended Topaz High School for part of my high school education. I participated in student government activities and played varsity football. I relocated to Chicago and completed my high school education there. I went on to attend Elmhurst College for two years. I went to an optometry school and received a degree. I worked for an ophthalmologist for many years. The last twenty years I devoted full-time to my own practice in Skokie, Illinois, until my retirement.

YAYOE MATSUSHITA MATSUURA

Current Residence: San Francisco, California
Prewar Residence: San Francisco, California

My father came to America before the 1906 earthquake and fire. I think he had to escape to the Golden Gate Park. My father worked for a *hakujin* family. He went back to Japan to marry my mother because they were not doing picture bride weddings anymore. My mother came to America around 1921 or 1922.

My mother took us to Japan when I was three years old, and I came back to San Francisco when I was twelve years old just before the war. I did not speak English and so it was difficult to make friends. I think they wanted to go back to Japan to live there and so they thought it was important for us to have a Japanese education.

Our prewar address was 214 Clement Street. I went to the George Peabody Elementary School. I didn't speak English, so they put me in the third grade to learn to read and write English. That was not easy, but the math was too easy for me because I was twelve years old.

On December 7th I was at the Sunday School at the Soko Ji temple. We couldn't believe it. We didn't know where Pearl Harbor was.

My father died after we came back from Japan so he didn't go to camp. My family and I were bused to the

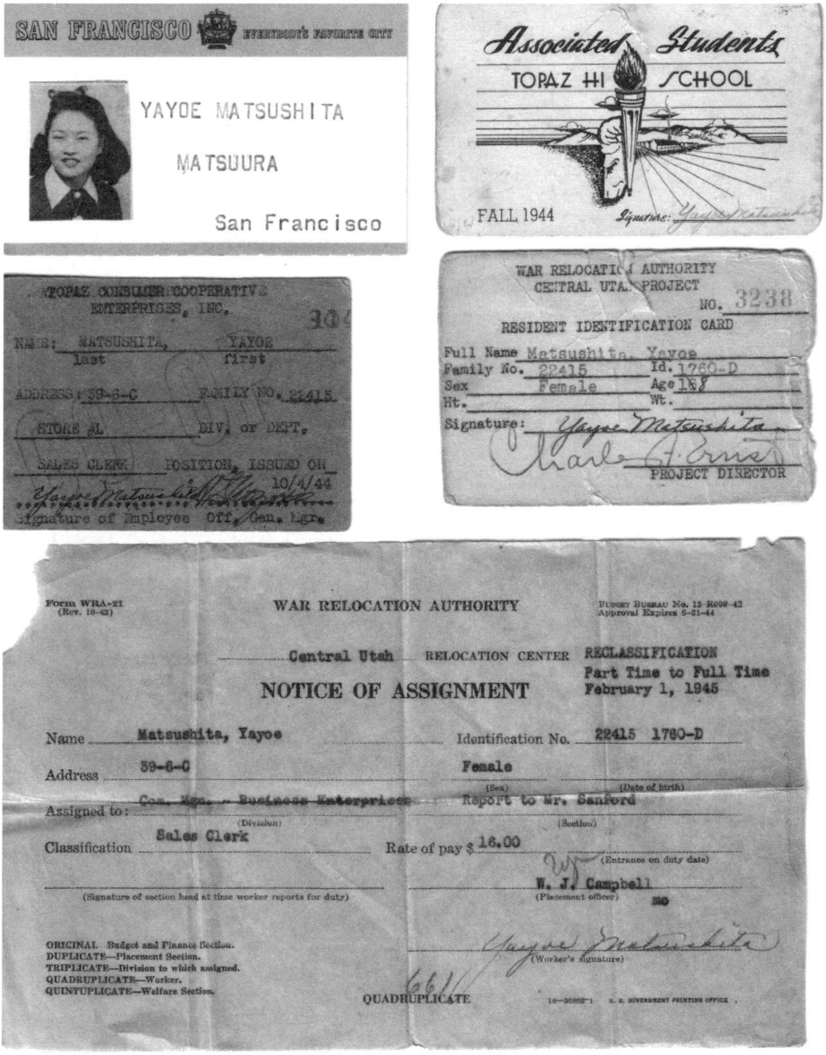

SAN FRANCISCO EVERYBODY'S FAVORITE CITY

YAYOE MATSUSHITA

MATSUURA

San Francisco

Associated Students

TOPAZ HI SCHOOL

FALL 1944 Signature: Yayoe Matsushita

TOPAZ CONSUMER COOPERATIVE
ENTERPRISES, INC. 104

NAME: MATSUSHITA, YAYOE
last first

ADDRESS: 39-6-C FAMILY NO. 22415

STORE #L DIV. or DEPT.

SALES CLERK POSITION, ISSUED ON 10/4/44

Yayoe Matsushita

Signature of Employee Off. Gen. Mgr.

WAR RELOCATION AUTHORITY
CENTRAL UTAH PROJECT
NO. 3238

RESIDENT IDENTIFICATION CARD

Full Name Matsushita, Yayoe
Family No. 22415 Id. 1760-D
Sex Female Age 18
Ht. Wt.
Signature: Yayoe Matsushita

Charles F. Ernst
PROJECT DIRECTOR

Form WRA-21
(Rev. 10-42)

WAR RELOCATION AUTHORITY

Budget Bureau No. 13-R009-42
Approval Expires 6-31-44

Central Utah RELOCATION CENTER

RECLASSIFICATION
Part Time to Full Time
February 1, 1945

NOTICE OF ASSIGNMENT

Name Matsushita, Yayoe Identification No. 22415 1760-D

Address 39-6-C Female
(Sex) (Date of birth)

Assigned to: Com. Mgn. - Business Enterprises Report to Mr. Sanford
(Division) (Section)

Classification Sales Clerk Rate of pay $ 16.00
(Entrance on duty date)

(Signature of section head at time worker reports for duty)

W. J. Campbell
(Placement officer) MO

ORIGINAL Budget and Finance Section.
DUPLICATE—Placement Section.
TRIPLICATE—Division to which assigned.
QUADRUPLICATE—Worker.
QUINTUPLICATE—Welfare Section.

Yayoe Matsushita
(Worker's signature)

661

QUADRUPLICATE

16—30862-1 U. S. GOVERNMENT PRINTING OFFICE

Yayoe's Topaz Memorabilia

Tanforan Assembly Center in San Bruno, California. We were assigned a barracks that was still under construction in the infield track. We sat and waited with our suitcases and bags in front of our assigned barracks. I saw doors cut and walls being put up. The upper part of the barracks were entirely open to the air. You could hear whispering two or three doors away. Weeds grew up between the floorboards. My mother, my sister, my brother and I were assigned to one room. We lived in Block 39, Barracks 5 C. Leftover wood pieces were scattered about outside. We gathered those wood pieces to use as kindling.

Just prior to being evacuated, we had purchased sleeping bags expressly for the evacuation. We carried our sleeping bags, with our blankets and sheets rolled inside and placed them on the metal frame beds. Later on, at Topaz, those sleeping bags really helped to keep us warm during the cold winters.

On the train ride to Topaz, there were a group of *Kibei* boys who were assigned to the same block as my family and me. My brother became friends with them.

Impressions of Topaz: Sagebrush, wind sandstorms. Everything covered with a powdcry dust, like ashes. Although the windows and doors were closed tight, everything was covered with a whitish powder of sand. I remember when a friend used a bucket and mop and helped us clean our floor after a sandstorm. The scorpions looked like dried shrimp coming out of the dusty ground.

I didn't participate in school activities very much because my English was not very good. The teachers I remember having were Miss Lyle for history, Mrs. Robinson for Spanish, Mr. Maggiora for shorthand, and Mr. Kusunoki for tailoring. I enjoyed Mr. Maggiora's shorthand class very much. I love to sew, so I especially liked Mr. Kusunoki's tailoring class. I made a regular suit in class. I did tailoring

The Canteen

for the first time and I made my own pattern measuring my size. I remember some girls made overcoats.

There was a English class for *Kibei,* and I hung around with girls from that class. The teachers were Miss Suyemoto and Mrs. Kitamura. It was an Adult Ed class for *Issei* and *Kibei.* They had day classes and evening classes. I took an evening typing class at the administration building, using the typewriters after the office was closed.

I worked part time at the Co-op store. Then in the summer I got part-time work at the administration canteen. I was paid $8.00 per month. Then I moved to the camp canteen because it was closer. I was a sales clerk for the magazines and things. They sold some Japanese food, too. If you worked full time, you got paid $16.00 a month.

When I came back from camp, my sister and I worked as domestics with this family. I was the upstairs maid, and my sister was the cook and worked downstairs. Later on, I worked for Mr. and Mrs. Schwartz on 7th Avenue, and my sister worked for a family nearby on 7th Avenue, too.

YOSHI HARAMAKI MILLER

Current Residence: Oakland, California
Prewar Residence: Hayward, California

We didn't hear about Pearl Harbor until the afternoon. On Sunday afternoons or evenings we used to listen to the radio. That's what we did. We would sit around the radio and listen to *The Aldrich Family.* That's when we heard it, and it really was kind of scary because we didn't know what it really meant. We were scared to go to school. I had just started high school and I didn't like high school anyway. I think I was scared, but I don't remember our neighbors saying anything. I guess they wouldn't be telling me about it, but maybe they might be talking to my father about it.

I guess we came in big buses or trucks from Delta. I said, "Gee, we're way out in the sticks." We lived w-a-a-y out in block 36, w-a-a-y out in the corner. The showers were only at certain places at the beginning. I can remember my mother getting lost and going in the other direction. Instead of coming to 36, she was kitty corner, way at the other end. Taking a shower, I remember there was no privacy there either. It was hard.

At home we had to be quiet, so being a nurse's aide after school I spent all of my time at the hospital. I worked in surgery. A person that I admired was Masae Mori. She was a registered nurse. There weren't that many nurses. She graduated from Stanford Lane Hospital in San Francisco. I remember the doctors were Dr. [James] Goto, and there was a shy doctor, Dr. [John] Teshima. Dr. [Henry} Sugiyama came from Sacramento and I didn't know him that well. And there was a [Dr. Paul] Yamauchi. So they were the few doctors that I knew. I remember Masae Mori. I think she had some key people helping. I don't remember nurses at all. She must have taught the older people to be in charge and then Masae would be in charge of them.

My parents weren't alive when the reparation money came. That was too bad. At that time they said you could send in the same form and you got the apology. So I got that for my father and mother. The *Sansei* really did a good job. They kept at it. You have to admire those kids. There weren't that many *Nisei*, except for that Korematsu and a few others. I remember Korematsu because he was from San Lorenzo. Most people didn't know how to fight things like this. I didn't know what it was. But Korematsu having a girlfriend made a difference. He really wanted to be with his girlfriend.

But these young kids: They have more political savvy, where we went along with what they said. Even in school, what they said was the truth. Now you find out you can't believe anyone. You can't trust anyone. And these kids already had that savvy. I'm finally getting to understand these kinds of things. I thought people that you liked, you just believed them. Not any more! Now I even go on strike. I'm sure they're taking pictures of people. I go to the Mothers Against Drunk Driving, or to anything where I could make another body to make it look better.

As soon as they act against the war, I'm going to be there. I have too many things on my mind, but those are the things I go to. Like against the police thing. I go up there and I think that's one extra person, an old lady, an Asian. They think that it's just Black people that are complaining. There're a lot of people, but they're too busy working, or they can't walk. But I have my health and I can go represent these people.

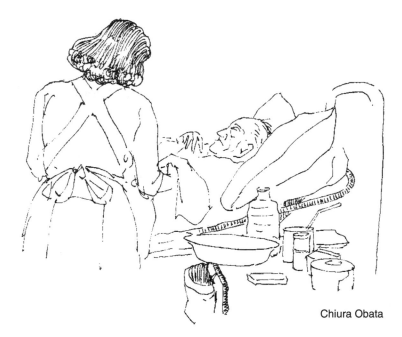

Chiura Obata

Nurse's Aide in Hospital

TERUYO "TERRY" TAMURA MITSUYOSHI

Current Residence: San Jose, California
Prewar Residence: Redwood City, California

Most of my friends were Japanese from the Horgan Ranch community. Everyday after we got out of regular school, we went to Japanese school. In those days, the Japanese kids had little interaction with *hakujin* kids. We had a close-knit family with two younger sisters and were quite content with life.

On December 7th my two sisters and I were at the movies in Redwood City. I can't recall what movie was playing, but they stopped the film and the lights went on and they made the announcement that Japan had attacked Pearl Harbor. I was so scared. But being the oldest, I couldn't show my fear to my younger sisters. I took each of them by the hand and we walked home as we could. I kept looking around to see if there was anything threatening.

The next day, I went to school and there were no problems that I can remember except that Kiyo and Kenji Yamane who lived near us rode a tandem bicycle to school and someone loosened some screws, so on the way home the bike collapsed and they fell off. I suspect sabotage. But other than that incident, I don't recall any other.

Several months later, the FBI came to our house to interrogate my father. One FBI agent even looked into the ice trays of the refrigerator. As I was the oldest, I took it upon myself to ask the man what he was looking for. He answered, "Maybe your father has something hidden in the trays." I will never forget that. There was another agent who kept saying that everything was going to be all right. They started to take my father away and I asked, "Where are you taking him?" They answered, "To the Redwood City jail." That was the last time we saw him until his release. My father was a quiet, unassuming man and was apolitical. Evidently, the reason they arrested him was that he had been contributing money to a charitable organization in Japan. A lot of families were doing that. It was a sad day for us.

I got clothes from the catalogs, Sears and Montgomery Wards. We enjoyed looking at the catalogs and called them our "wish books." I didn't wear jeans or have any fancy hairdos. I don't know if they even had a beauty shop there. I didn't know anyone who smoked. I think if you don't have any brothers in the family, you live a very sheltered life. My mother also told us that Japanese girls never get pregnant before they were married. But I saw a number of single girls who were pregnant in Topaz. It was another myth that went by the wayside.

My mother tried to make the barracks as livable as possible. We had benches around the potbelly stove and had a little area where we made snacks. One of the mainstays of our diet was Spam. The food in the mess hall was terrible. They served a lot of stewed stuff—unidentified meat with rice. And then there was Jello. It was very hard. So whenever the food was unappetizing at the mess hall,

Army-Style Meals in Mess Hall

we would make cocoa and eat some Spam. I do not like Spam to this day except Spam *musubi*s [rice balls] made by Jay Sasagawa. He makes the best Spam *musubi*s. I went to the Aldersgate Methodist Church Bazaar and asked for some Spam *musubi* made by Jay and they were all sold out. I don't know his secret of making Spam *musubi*s.

We returned to California before most of the others left in camp. We found a place in Woodside near Redwood City, where my father worked as a gardener and took care of one horse. My mother was a domestic worker. It was right across from the old Woodside store and it was nice to be back in California.

However, there was one ugly incident: My sisters and I went to San Francisco and walked down Market Street and stopped in a restaurant to have a hamburger. A Filipino busboy came up to the waitress and said, "Don't serve them because they are a bunch of Japs." I was the oldest, so I just wanted to get out of there. But the waitress said to just sit there and she would bring us our hamburgers. She was the nicest person.

At the time of the evacuation, I felt that the government did this to protect us. There were stories of Japanese being shot at in Coyote and that brought a lot of fear to the Japanese community. I didn't give any thought as to the loss of civil liberties that happened. As I look back on the evacuation now, I get angry that my father was taken from us for no good reason. I get angry for the way that my parents had to suffer. I get angry that I didn't have the opportunity to go to college. I feel that the 1942 to 1945 time period was lost and I have blocked out most of the memories.

I did learn one new thing from the camp experience: Mama always said that Japanese were better than everyone else, but don't bring shame to the family. In camp, I never saw so many Japanese people and I was overwhelmed. In spite of my mother's best intentions, I found that Japanese people were the same as anyone else. There were good and bad people; they did good things as well as bad. We were not the superior race.

ISAMU MOMII

Current Residence: University Place, Washington
Prewar Residence: Alameda, California

There were many Japanese families in Alameda and I was very comfortable there.

I went to Japanese school every day after going to the regular school. Since I went to Japanese school every day and had close proximity to Japanese families, most of my friends were Japanese, but [I] did have a few Caucasian friends.

I can't remember what I was doing on December 7th, but when I heard about Pearl Harbor I was shocked and a little ashamed. The next day at school was filled with apprehension, but I can't recall any adverse incidents. About twenty-five percent of the class was Japanese. Because of the proximity of the Navy base in Alameda, all Japanese aliens had to move out of the immediate area. My parents were aliens so our family moved to the Centerville area.

I can remember a few teachers at Topaz High: A Mrs. Plummer, who taught English; Shinji Momono, who taught math; and a George Suzuki, who taught drafting. The education was barely adequate, but I adapted to the program and did what I had to. I did enjoy the drafting and math classes. I wasn't the *yogore* [dirty; bad boy] type and not a joiner. I did not join any clubs and I wasn't into sports. My most mischievous act was climbing the water tower. I do remember working at the commissary unloading trucks.

I think I went to a few dances, but I wore regular clothes, no pegged pants or zoot suits. I didn't have a ducktail hairdo. It just wasn't my style. There was one fellow. We called him Mop, Mop Fukuoka. He had a lot of long hair and wore pegged pants.

I can't recall what I felt about the evacuation at the time. I do feel a little resentment now. I am sort of angry that we lost our civil rights and that was hard to take. But it was the Japanese way of *shikata ga nai.* The reparations were small compensation for the trials that we went through and I regret that my parents did not receive anything.

There was one aspect of the evacuation that I felt was good for me. It made me adapt to changes and adverse situations. It gave me more resolve and determination. The camp experience introduced me to a lot of new friends and we all shared the same experiences. I go to as many reunions as possible to maintain these friendships.

Hi-Y Boys Club

ALICE AIKO NOMURA MORITA

Current Residence: Granada Hills, California
Prewar Residence: Oakland, California

I was born on January 2, 1928 in Sacramento, California. I was married to Roy Morita of San Jose. He passed away on November 14, 1984. He was a cartoonist for Jay Ward Productions and created *Rocky & Bullwinkle*.

My father (Harry Hiroshi Morita), being a *Nisei*, owned the house we lived in. We lived downstairs and rented the upstairs. A large Chinese family lived next door. The Oakland Japanese ME Church was just a couple of blocks away. However, our family attended the Layman's Church in Berkeley. The Nakanos (Mitsu Asaoka's family) and Takahashis (Sachi Doi and Mako's family) were also members of the church. At the outbreak of the war, the only racist experience I can remember were derogatory remarks made by a hateful Filipino girl who lived down the street.

Prior to evacuation we stored most of our family furnishings in a shed in back of the house. The Chinese people that lived next door said they would watch over our stuff and my dad left them some of his gardening equipment. Needless to say, when we returned from Topaz (via Chicago) to Oakland, much of the stored items were ransacked.

If my memory serves me correctly, we walked to the Greyhound Bus Station [in Oakland] for the evacuation bus. There were stories going around that we would be housed in Alcatraz, but we didn't know where we were going. The bus took us to Tanforan Assembly Center and to the horse-stall home, which was dirty, smelly, and intolerable. Our family of eight was assigned two stalls!

In Tanforan, the only thing I can remember was we were always waiting in line for food, shots, and school in the grandstands. I enjoyed the talent shows, especially with Goro Suzuki. His brother Mickey was a grammar school classmate of mine. My father worked in the commissary at Tanforan, but he felt betrayed by the government for locking him up in a place like this. The food was awful; seems like we had mush everyday.

The journey to Topaz was uneventful. My father and five girls, with Flora getting motion sickness all the way to Delta. My mother (Haruko Furukawa, born in Yamaguchi-ken) died of heart failure just before the war began. My brother Paul relocated to Sandy, Utah, where my sister Hilda and her husband had relocated to. I think my father wanted to make sure Paul received a good education in an outside high school. We lived in Block 12-2-C/D in Topaz. The Nakasos, Yoshimoris, Ashizawas, and Moris all lived in the same block. Although the environment was dirty and dusty, I had fun as a teenager. We wore mackinaws and bandannas like everyone else.

History was my favorite subject in high school. I liked Frank Sinatra's singing and I listened to the *Hit Parade* a lot. Our family relocated to Chicago in my senior year at Topaz. I attended Hyde Park High School. The community and school were predominantly Jewish. School was especially tough. In February 1946, we returned to Oakland from Chicago via train.

Although I've lost track of her, my pal in Topaz was Mich (Hiratsuka) Nishino Yamane. She went to Tule Lake, but I last heard she was in Reno.

My father probably had the greatest influence on me. He was a strict disciplinarian (he had to be with a family of six girls) and I respected him and admired him for his strength and fortitude.

MARY TAMAKI MURAKAMI

Current Residence: Bethesda, Maryland
Prewar Residence: San Francisco, California

We lived in San Francisco Japantown and could not believe that war had broken out that fateful day in December until the Army surrounded our neighborhood. It was ironic because my father would not start his vegetable business after we had moved to San Francisco because he had said that Japan was going to go to war against America. After that day, the curfew affected our family by curtailing the area of travel. My sister had to quit work and come home from Atherton, my brother could not go to school, and my father could not go to work. Finally, in April, I had to leave high school.

My sister Lily was in one of the first groups to go to Topaz and was able to get our family of seven two smaller rooms instead of one larger room. My parents and my brother were in one room and the girls were in the other. It was a tough life, especially for our parents, until we settled into a routine. I helped my father build furniture, put up sheetrock walls, carry coal, and learned how to keep the fire going in the potbelly stove.

Since I turned sixteen in June, I was able to go to work in a cannery near Ogden. The living conditions there were worse than in camp. But we were free. When the cannery closed, we worked on the farms picking crops. The work was too hard to work a full day for us. We would quit after a half day and rest. This would annoy the farmer and the Japanese workers who were not from Topaz.

One Japanese worker said to me that I should have a hat since the sun was so strong. I told him I did not have one and could not get to town to buy one. The next day he brought me a new hat to wear. I never forgot his kindness. Although most of these Japanese thought we were lazy, we tried to explain to them that we were originally from cities and had never worked on a farm.

We had an academically poor high school education, but we overcame that by our own diligence. We had fun and good memories, overcame bad ones and we should be proud of our accomplishments in integrating back into the American society. Only people who shared this period of our lives would understand the friendship we share with our classmates.

My father was ill for awhile in camp from exhaustion of the evacuation and his family. Redress and reparations came too late for *Issei*, who endured the most of the hardships during the war years. I have discussed the internment experience with my children and friends and still feel strongly about being questioned about our loyalty with the "yes-yes" and "no- no" answers. I do not feel it was right that my brother was drafted out of camp and we had to stand on the other side of the fence to see him leave for the Army.

EMI NAGASAWA

Current Residence: Sacramento, California
Prewar Residence: Sacramento, California

On December 7, 1941—Pearl Harbor Day—we were at the Buddhist Church *kaikan* [hall] and I was either watching or playing basketball. I remember there was a lot of excitement and noise and there were some US military soldiers in Japantown. I think we were called because everyone went rushing out. That's when I heard about Pearl Harbor. I didn't think too much about it. I was too young. My parents didn't say anything about that day.

On the day of our evacuation, we gathered at the Memorial Building right around J Street. That was not a Japanese building. We went by bus to report to the Wallerga Assembly Center right here in Sacramento. I didn't know our destination. Don't recall any of our friends being on the bus. I don't know if Wallerga was a park; it was a temporary shelter. We lived in barracks. They had mess halls. I don't remember anything about the food they served there because when I was young I didn't eat. Even in Topaz I never went to the mess hall because I had no one to eat with. My parents were working in the mess hall. At first I would eat with my brothers—and once they got to know other people they reserved a whole table for themselves and that left me out. My mom would bring my food home. I was a very fussy eater and since I didn't have anyone to eat with, I just didn't eat.

We started school at Topaz shortly after we arrived there in September of 1943. I didn't think too much one way or the other about the Topaz kids because we had our gang from Tule there. To me, it didn't make any difference. Maybe we were stared at, but I can't recall that they were not friendly.

I enjoyed sports. I remember traveling to a few places to play basketball: Wasatch Academy, Delta, and maybe Hinckley. We always won, although they were bigger and taller and we were much smaller.

In Topaz, the first-string team in basketball was Bubbles and Abu Keikoan, and Aki Sato, Joanna and Natalie Nakamura, Nancy Takahashi, and me. We got to know Nancy after we were in Topaz because her sister married an Okamoto from Sacramento. I think our coach was Yosh Isono. In Topaz, there were no other teams to compete with, whereas in Tule Lake there were many teams. In baseball, even the blocks had their own teams so there was a lot of competition there. There were some block teams for girls. We used to play baseball in a field near the high school gym. I recall playing a girls' team from Delta. Some people made an ice rink near us and I tried ice skating.

I never walked out of a class or did anything disruptive. There were several guys who were kinda bad. The teacher would make a statement and these guys would say, "How come?" and then it was, "Why?" They would then ask more questions to harass her. Nothing really bad.

It was people like Wacky, and the kids would laugh at all these crazy antics.

My nickname is "Wyno." It came about when I was playing ball in a park in Sacramento. My Mexican neighbor around the corner, but I don't know for what reason, started to call me "Wyno." Everybody called me by that name all during camp. No one calls me that anymore, except when I run into old camp friends who don't know that I now go by my real name, Emi.

Being the only girl, it was very difficult because I had to learn everything on my own. My mother wouldn't even tell me—and I laugh about it now—about local gossip that some *Issei* man was fooling around with some woman. It seems like the *Issei* were doing things like that all the time. She would tell my sister-in-law, but never tell me anything like that. Maybe she thought I shouldn't hear stories like that. We were too innocent in Topaz, very protected. Sometimes I'm shocked by what I hear, but I really don't like to gossip. I never had that curiosity.

I look back on the internment years and the best thing was that I made a lot of friends. I don't feel any real anger about the internment because I don't talk about it. But sometimes I do get upset when I look back and realize what happened to us. I was really too young at the time to give the internment serious thought.

HIROKAZU "CLEM" NAKAI

Current Residence: Roseville, California
Prewar Residence: San Francisco, California

For three years our address was 6-3-C: Block 6, Barracks 3, Room C. That was 6-3-C. My father Mitsuru, from Ehime-ken, died at age fifty-five of apoplexy in Topaz when I was fourteen or fifteen. Because these *Issei* used to work twelve hours a day, I hardly saw him except for dinner time. I really didn't know him that good.

I knew Juji "Joker" Hada from Konko Church in Japantown. We went to Roosevelt Junior High School together, too. When we went to Topaz, we started to mingle with each other once high school started there. We used to just clown around a lot. Juji acquired the name "Joker" at Topaz. On V-E Day [Victory in Europe] we had an assembly in the auditorium and we acted out the victory. One time we took part in a skit that the drama class had, "The Gay Nineties Review."

I used to hum the song that played when the Clem Kadiddlehopper character played by Red Skelton appeared on the radio. One day, this fellow named Bill Sakai started calling me "Clem" because I kept humming that all the time. I haven't been able to get rid of that nickname, but I don't mind.

We used to ad lib skits after picking a subject. Joker was the "straight man," like Dean Martin was to Jerry Lewis. I had to come up with the funny parts. I remember doing *naniwa bushi,* which is Japanese singing, while Joker would come in during the lines and make something funny out of it. I often wondered what the Caucasian teachers thought while we were doing it. I got the idea for the skit from going to Japanese movies at Kinmon Gakuen (Golden Gate Japanese School) before the war, where in between scenes we would hear these narrators [*benshi*] break in sometimes and they'd sing like that telling you something about the story. (That school still exists on Bush near Buchanan.) I think the skits helped the students forget that they were in camp for that moment. Doing comedy, I made friends in camp. Otherwise, I would have been a "loner." I was among friends at that time.

In camp, the girls I went around with and the one I ended up marrying were all basketball players. And I could hardly play basketball myself. Those girls went out to the surrounding communities like Delta, Fillmore, and Hinckley to play against Caucasian basketball teams. Both of the girls I used to go with in camp live in Sacramento. One was Bubbles Keikoan. Wyno Nagasawa, too. Neither one of them ever got married. At one time, I had a crush on Kumi Ishida. Nothing came of it; it was just one-sided. I had a crush on June Yamada, too. She was two or three classes below.

About the only place you could go was the movies. Topaz had a co-op and from the money they made there, they got these movies to show in the recreation hall. They had two rows of flat benches, but everyone else—there were 200 or 300 people—sat on the floor.

Joker and Clem

There was a Frank Shimamoto, a *Nisei*. There was friction between the *Nisei* and *Kibei* [U.S.-born, Japan-raised]. There used to be fistfights. It might have started as a gang fight, but it ended up with just those two guys. It ended up with Frank Shimamoto, who represented *Nisei*, fighting a *Kibei*. He always beat that other guy up. We'd hear that they were going meet each other at a certain corner, and then there would be gang of people there. And we'd watch them beat the heck out of each other. But it was the *Kibei* guy that always quit. The *Nisei* guy never lost, although he sure got some pretty bad bruises. That was another form of entertainment, you could say.

There was a *Kibei* named Hideo Nakai who had a grocery store in San Francisco. When they were going to be shipped to the camps, he had all his stock stored. He didn't just throw it away. Eventually, he had these canned goods shipped to the camp and sold it. It's his stuff, but I guess he profited from camp life.

The first liquor I had was in camp, Southern Comfort. Someone smuggled the bottle into camp and we would pass it around. I don't think anyone got drunk, because there were so many people there. We were still teenagers in high school. This wasn't an everyday thing. We might have had it before going to or at the school dances. Not all the time, whenever it was there.

The "Black-Out Dance" was where one light at a time goes out and it starts getting darker and darker. This took place in the dining hall. By the time it's dark you know that everybody's necking away with their girl or boy, you know? That's about the extent of it. You couldn't do anything else there. We didn't have a lot of the Black-Out Dances at first, but as we got older we had them more or less all the time. We had them at the proms, too, but only up to a point because there were chaperones.

I never tied in my private life up to now with the camp life, you know? I considered myself a loner until I went to high school in Topaz. I think for the first four or five years after we came back to San Francisco, everybody tried to see each other at these carnivals or bazaars that each town has. People would come back to see their old pals that they had made in Topaz. But, eventually, that fizzled out. But we still had a close relationship with the people we ran around with as a group. To this day, Joe Kimura calls me once a month. When he got married, his best man and grooms were friends from San Francisco. He was the best man at my wedding.

One time, Channel 4 in San Francisco interviewed me and Mas Kawaguchi about camp. He was maybe two grades higher than me in Topaz. He had more bitter things to talk about. I more or less kept my mouth shut and let him have his say because my views didn't match his. The first thing I did after receiving the reparations check was go to Sears to buy a stove, washing machine, and refrigerator. And I took my family on vacation to Hawaii. I made a photocopy of the check as a souvenir and kept the letter from President Bush.

Benny Nobori

JAMES MASAAKI NAKAMURA

Current Residence: San Francisco, California
Prewar Residence: Irvington, California

I went to school in Topaz for the entire three years of my high school. I remember the fat teacher, Mrs. Lisle, and she taught us Core. That was English, history, and social studies. I had Core, algebra with Eiko Hosoi. She was an excellent teacher. She caught me cheating once. I was sick for a week and I didn't know what we had covered, so I had to take the test. Evidently she caught me cheating because Jim Noda, who was very smart, said, "Here, copy my paper," which I did. But he made a mistake and I copied it. That's what gave me away. That was the only time I ever cheated and I got caught. I did not think I was that smart. I considered myself as just an average student. She didn't tell me directly about my cheating, but she did tell one of the guys in my block, Shig Nakayama. He was one of the helpers at the school. He helped the teachers. Anyway, Jim never said anything to me and I never said anything to him about the incident. We both knew it happened. All Shig said was that Miss Hosoi said, "One of the guys was cheating."

Education in Topaz was very interesting because all the subjects were new to me. I never studied; I was too lazy. Most of my friends were the same. We had tests in that physics class and they compared us against the national average, which was given at the beginning of the semester. At the end of the year they gave us the same test to see what we had learned. I'm not bragging, but I got the second highest score in the class. The teacher was very surprised because the three guys who got the highest scores sat together and he thought we were cheating. The other two guys were Jim Noda and Mike Ichimaru. The teacher did apologize for thinking that we were cheating. He said it was his mistake. At the final exam he purposely placed us apart from each other so we couldn't cheat. That was Anderson. Another classmate was Sotoi Kenmotsu. He was quiet but he was very smart. All the guys from Alameda were smart, like Sam Nakaso and Tohru Ota. I think the way that they taught school in Alameda was good because they taught the basics, everything from the bottom. They pounded this information into their heads. San Mateo kids were smart, too.

I went to most of the school dances. Tried to get a date every time. I used to have a crush on a Masako Tsuzuki. I think she's in New York. They used to play music from Glenn Miller, Benny Goodman, all the swing bands. I still listen to the music from the Big Band era.

I remember the school assemblies. My favorite entertainer was the comedian Joker Hada and his partner Clem Nakai. They were really funny. I also remember the professor from UCLA, Harry Kitano. He had a band and they were good. One band member was our classmate Kaz Maruoka. I remember Elsie Itashiki. She was a jazz singer and she was good. She passed away.

I worked for the agricultural department. I was a handyman, a helper, on the farm where they grew lots of vegetables for the camp. I didn't do much. There were about three of us classmates who worked there: Isao Baba, Tom Masuda, and I don't remember the other guy. I also worked for the commissary making deliveries to the mess halls. We worked in the afternoons because in the mornings we had to go to school. I worked there full time during the summer. I worked at the farm for one year. The guys in charge of the farm picked us up to go to work at the farm which was just outside the gate.

People talked about people who had sex. We were very innocent. I'll tell you a story: One of our family friends who was still in high school got pregnant. She had her baby in camp. It was embarrassing for the family because everyone knew about it.

Dance Bids

I went to the senior prom with Masako Tsuzuki, but we didn't enjoy it. She dropped me and started to go around with someone else. We went to the ball together, but she already had another guy. That happened at the Sophomore Hop because she went to that dance with that guy. I found out and told her I didn't want to take her to the senior ball, but she said I had to. You know, when you're young, things like that happen.

Our class of Topaz 1945 was an experience you can't forget, especially the people you grew up with. Classmates are interesting. Our class reunions are okay. My wife is Japanese-speaking and she has met Rosie Kumekawa's wife and also Henry Nakamura's wife and I think she would enjoy the reunion as she could talk to them, too. We will attend the class dinner on August 31. It will be good to see everybody.

SAM WILLIAM NAKASO

Current Residence: San Jose, California
Prewar Residence: Alameda, California

On December 7th, I felt no difference with my friends. They were cordial, and there was one friend who was a foot taller than me, and I had to look up to him to talk, but we got along very well as before. My mother told us of one incident when she was on the bus coming home from work and was harassed by a man. The bus driver intervened and told the man to be quiet or get off the bus. I always felt that Alameda was a nice, friendly, peaceful place.

The train ride to Topaz was boring and I was just wishing that it would end soon. It was close quarters and I do not remember many details. Some friends say that the cars had gaslights, but I can't recall. I do remember that we ate, but it was not a memorable meal. We arrived in Delta and we were treated like cattle, herded from one place to another. It was hot and dusty and I was amazed at how light the alkaline soil was as we stepped into the dusty, inches-deep soil that was to be home for some undetermined time.

I was not much of a student and was not serious about school. In retrospect I wish I had taken advantage of some of the good teachers there. The J.A. teachers stand out in my mind, like Norm Hirose did an outstanding job. There was Rose-something—she taught math and was good. Then there was a Caucasian teacher who I gave a bad time. She taught English and I kept asking her what good all of this was going to do for me later. I can remember writing an essay in her class. It was about a fellow who was sitting on a mountainside and contemplating suicide looking at the sunset and all that. She and I had a long talk about that.

In Topaz, there were a lot of opportunities to play high school sports for everyone that may not have been available in their previous schools. There were many good athletes and after I left camp, I would think of Tom Tomioka and all those San Francisco guys. I would also think about Sus Ota, the softball player, and Lefty Honda the baseball player. Then there was Min Ota, who was an up-and-coming athlete when the war broke out.

I don't remember many memorable assemblies at school, but there was one: The Clem and Joker act stands out. They were funny and I think it was important to have something that made the students laugh and enjoy. I did go to dances but wasn't dating anyone and wasn't interested in dating. I do remember some of the popular recording artists: Glenn Miller, Woody Herman, Frank Sinatra, Bob Crosby, Bing Crosby, Harry James and "Song of India," "Moonlight Serenade," "Two O'Clock Jump," "Tangerine." I made a lot of new friends and many had nicknames: "Wacky" (he was a little wacky) and "Ratcho." (I think it came from his name Richard). "Chinky," because he looked like a Chinaman to me. "Clem," since he was part of the Clem and Joker combo like Red Skelton and

Clem Kadiddlehopper. His real name is Hirokazu. "Joker" was part of the comedy team.

Some of the fads of the time were ducktail hairdos slicked down with Three Flower pomade that really had an aroma. I think it is still on the market. There were the zoot suits and pants that were pegged, very narrow at the cuffs. The Sacto [Sacramento] fellas came to camp some wore zoot suits. My brother had pegged pants and occasionally I wore them even if they didn't fit. I don't know of anyone who drank alcohol or smoked. In Alameda, we would sit behind the building at Japanese school and smoke. We would pick up butts from the street and smoke them. I don't think the kids today can relate to that.

My sister was teaching Japanese at Yale in New Haven, Connecticut, so at the end of my junior year of high school, my other sister Betty and I went East with the idea that I would finish high school in New Haven. On the way, we stopped at the train station and I saw one of the Yano boys from camp and he was in an Army uniform. Strange coincidence to see him there. In New Haven, we were tolerated with no incidences of outward discrimination. Many years later, my sister told me that her hairdresser said that her daughter had told her that "Mom, we have a new student in our class and I think he is an Indian," talking about me, of course. I tried to be part of the community, going to school and finding a summer job.

On my way to New Haven, I stopped in New York City to visit Kenzo Ishimaru and suggested that he come along with me to New Haven to look the place over. He did and he liked the area so we both enrolled at Hillhouse High School. I think going to New Haven to finish my high school education helped me getting through college. The Topaz interlude was not the best.

I am personally not bitter about the internment experience. I never did reflect back on it to see if it was an advantage or not. When I became an adult, I realized that the internment opened the door for many, many *Niseis*—opportunity for employment, opportunity to use their education. I remember a fellow who married a girl from Alameda: Ki Nomura was from Berkeley and he married Ellie Akamatsu, and he couldn't find a job and had to go gardening. I thought that was a terrible deal, going to college and not being able to find a job. I think those that found jobs had to go to San Francisco and hook up with a Japanese firm. There were not many openings because everyone from the Bay Area was looking for work. So the internment opened the door to go back East. I had some doubts about taking the reparations money, but after some thought I accepted it and banked it. I saw a documentary on KQED [public broadcasting station] the other day about the evacuation and it made me angry. I taped it and am going to give it to my daughter. She wasn't interested a few years ago, but now she is.

We went by the Topaz campsite the other year and there is a family living across from there. We asked where the camp was and they said right across the road. There is a plaque there denoting the spot and there are bullet holes in it.

DWIGHT KEN NISHIMURA

Current Residence: Houston, Texas
Prewar Residence: Berkeley, California

We lived in Berkeley before the war and I remember December 7 very vividly. I had gone to Sunday school like all good preachers' kids do. There was this Black kid who came ambling across a vacant lot next door to tell me, "It's too bad that your country has gone to war against mine!" I felt it strange that he put things in that perspective. I can remember the notices posted on the telephone poles that stated the restrictions on our travels. I can recall the people who were taken into custody by the authorities.

At Topaz, the rec hall became a new part of our vocabulary and we spent many hours there. Kids were bored, so many new forms of entertainment sprung up: dancing, cards, and all those other sinful activities. In hindsight, I have learned to appreciate what our elders did in getting the camp organized: order, discipline, governance, school. Henry Tani was instrumental in establishing the school. There were those many volunteers that were teaching for the first time: Katherine Nakaso, Eiko Hosoi Katayama, Rose "Miss Cotton-Pot" Watanabe to name a few. I have always been grateful that they stepped into the breach. There were so many unsung heroes and heroines.

The dust of Topaz was unforgettable. It was everywhere. It was everywhere. The total absence of anything green was overwhelming. The barbed wire, the symbolism of lost freedom never got to me. This was a lark, an adventure for a teenager, but total defeat for our parents. I don't think anyone ever got used to the latrines, mess halls ("meshi hole" as often heard from the *Issei*), the lines, and the dinner gong. That gong was like Pavlov running experiments in conditioned response.

School was always easy for me and we had a leg up on most Japanese families because we were surrounded by my father's good books. I am amazed that there was any learning at all between the lack of books and the primitive facilities. We were so fortunate to have the likes of Eleanor Gerard and Doc Goodman. When one thinks about all those remarkable people that came out to help us, we can only feel blessed.

I could hear my parents talking after they thought we were asleep. They were concerned that the family authority was breaking down. We kids didn't look to them for anything. We wanted to wear those pea coats like everyone else. Occasionally, I wanted to be more of a *yogore*—a juvenile delinquent—because they seemed to have more fun. All of this did not sit well with my parents.

Friendships which I made from camp are to be treasured, but one needs to work at maintaining them. I call a few of my old friends periodically. I live in Houston now and if I were in California perhaps my need to see all of the friends would be greater. I feel I have a pretty good balance.

Redress has come and gone. We deserved it, but it was not enough. If we discounted twenty thousand bucks back to1942, we would be getting a mere pittance. As for the evacuation, if we had more experience and if we were more numerous such affronts to our rights and dignity would not have taken place. My kids find this all very confusing. My grandchildren will be totally uninformed. Times change and new issues surface. The most we can do as individuals is to fight injustice around us and keep eternally vigilant.

SOMAO OCHI

Current Residence: San Francisco, California
Prewar Residence: San Francisco, California

Before we were removed to Topaz, furnishings offered to neighbors were pounced upon, vulture-like. Some valuable antiques and art works from my deceased father's art repair business that had been placed in storage at the San Francisco Buddhist Church gym were plundered during our incarceration. Missing was a crate of his paintings. I do not recall any overt negative treatment from my friends and neighbors with one exception. A "friend" from a Chinese laundry nearby had scrawled on our stairway in Chinese characters *Nihon o tao-se* ("Defeat Japan").

A few grade school friends from Pacific Heights School came to see us at Tanforan. One young Caucasian visitor was a close friend who went to Japanese language school with the rest of us Japanese kids after regular school let out. He was close to the Japanese community. There was an area beneath the grandstand called the visitor center where internees could meet with visitors from the outside. We just mostly stood around self consciously, not knowing what to say.

I secretly looked forward to going to this place somewhere in the desert. Heretofore, the farthest I had ever traveled from San Francisco was the fifty miles to San Jose. To me, a fourteen-year-old, this was an adventure. The hardships awaiting us were merely part of the adventure. Adding to the evacuees' fears was a rumor that one of the earlier evacuees, well known to most of us, was stung by a scorpion and had died. Luckily, waiting to greet us upon our arrival at Topaz was the "victim," Koji Urabe!

Rumor had it that the Army guards were specially selected "Section Eights," i.e., eligible for early discharge for possessing low IQs and/or for having undesirable behavior problems. One had to be very careful not to stray too close to the fence for they were apt to have itchy trigger fingers. In Topaz, one such elderly stroller was shot to death by a guard.

Many residents handcrafted *geta* (wooden Japanese clogs) from scrap wood. The *geta* proved to be a great innovation for slogging through mud and snow, as well as when used for showering. *Geta*-making became an art form of sorts with residents turning out everything from crude *geta* made from scrap two-by fours with rope thongs to elegantly designed ones beautifully hand-painted and varnished.

I've often wondered why Topaz didn't have a "regular" school building like certain other camps like Heart Mountain, for example. Our school was no different than the barracks occupied by the residents. Each apartment room was used as a classroom. I remember having chemistry in the laundry room. I also remember getting caught cheating in Miss Sundquist's advanced algebra class getting answers from a classmate. I felt bad that he had his paper taken away too.

When I was in the ninth grade, I was embarrassed having to wear a sweater to school that was knitted by my mother that appeared to have puffed sleeves that made me look all the more "dorky." I pretty much wore the same clothes, mostly from Sears, day in and day out. On the first day of school, I counted two others in my biology class with the same long-sleeved plaid shirt from Sears. I felt pretty good because there were others that had the same taste, good or bad. The "cool" guys and those that could afford it wore Levi jackets and pants.

Imagine a camp mess hall dimly lit at night by two blue bulbs and teenagers dancing cheek-to-cheek to the music of Glenn Miller, when in comes an *ojisan* (father or man). He looks in stunned silence and then yells out, "*Nanda! Joro-ya mitaida!*" ("What the hell is this? A whore house?") Yeah, like the kind he frequented in Japan, I suppose.

I felt that *shikata ga nai* was the prevailing sentiment regarding our incarceration. You had to be mentally ill to be in denial during the internment years. Teenagers were generally more carefree and resilient than their *Issei* parents and older *Nisei*. The *Issei* and older *Nisei* had good reason to be angry because they were imprisoned during what should have been the most productive time of their lives in terms of education and employment. The loss of property and their freedom and the prospect of a dismal future must have caused many to be depressed.

Most *Issei* and *Nisei* didn't talk seriously about seeking redress. The prevailing thought was, "Forget redress. Let's get on with our lives." This thinking seems to be in line with the *Nisei* mentality that seeking monetary redress, would focus negative attention on Japanese Americans and that accepting money from the government was tantamount to an admission that this was adequate compensation for the misery and suffering brought on by internment. *Nisei* and *Issei* just sought a sense of normalcy in their long disrupted lives. Many didn't want old wounds reopened.

My wife and I visited Topaz in 1994. When we couldn't find the road that led to the Topaz site, we stopped at a house somewhere probably around Hinckley. The woman that came to the door said her husband, now deceased, taught animal husbandry at Topaz High and that they received a Christmas card every year from a former student. She asked if I knew a Dewey Fujii. Know him? We had classes together. Amazing coincidence!

Poking around in the Topaz soil, finding pieces of a ceramic mug, which I later glued back together, brought back a rush of memories from fifty years ago... 'nough to make one teary-eyed.

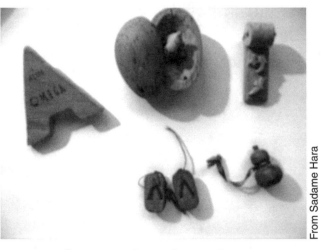

From Sadame Hara

Carvings from Scrap Lumber

DOROTHY S. HARADA ODA

Current Residence: El Cerrito, California
Prewar Residence: Oakland, California

Classes at Topaz High School were organized into low and high grades with teachers recruited however possible. That is, if one had at least a year of college or university, you could be a teacher. Interestingly, my geometry teacher, Asa Fujie, had attended the University of California, Berkeley for a year. As I learned much later, he was the best friend of my future husband who was at a different camp in Arkansas and was the best man at our wedding. The teacher of my French class was the wife of the commanding officer. Suffice it to say that she came to class not always prepared and we became quite proficient at singing "Frere Jacques" as a frequent lesson of the day.

Other teachers recruited from the outside were well qualified, such as Muriel Matzkin who was my physiology teacher and advisor to the Girl Reserves group. She was an inspiration to us all and even provided us with appropriate family-life education, as it is euphemistically called. Later, Miss Matzkin invited me to accompany her to the West Coast when anyone of Japanese ancestry could only travel there accompanied by a non-Japanese citizen.

Life and times at Topaz High had many of the attributes and activities of regular high schools due largely to the efforts of the students who tried to lead as "normal" a daily campus life as possible under quite atypical conditions. I will leave the recounting of accomplishments and tribulations to other students with better recall than mine. My own activities included singing in a trio with Chiyo Date Iino and Fumi Manabe Hayashi. The "Topaz Trio," as we were known, was sponsored and encouraged by our music teacher, Miss Barbara Loomis, who accompanied us on the piano.

I also joined an entertainment troupe as a ballet dancer, which I had studied to be for ten years. I was quite hesitant about performing outside of the protected camp, not knowing what kind of reception we would receive from the nearby townspeople; but, to my relief, they were welcoming and hospitable. I still remember fondly the delicious chicken and dumplings served to the performers by the people of Delta, a small rural town sixteen miles from Topaz. The costumes, as was my other limited wardrobe, were whatever my seamstress mother could fashion together from Sears Roebuck catalog orders.

In retrospect, our teen years at Topaz were turbulent as most adolescent years are. However, what defines our growing up as singularly unique was the space confinement, severely limited resources, externally controlled environment, lack of privacy, dense living quarters, and politically charged camp atmosphere that we could not escape. I believe we, as teenagers in the 1940s, were not as politically aware or socially conscious of civil rights as those living in present times rife with conflict throughout the world. Rightfully, we should have been outraged at the deprivations we suffered as individuals, families, and a targeted ethnic group. However, most of us were second-generation citizens existing between the dominant majority culture and traditional Japanese family and community ways in our merged and mixed lives. Our behavior, or lack of protest as teenagers, must be viewed in the context of the times. I make no excuses and point instead with pride in what we did with our lives to overcome what seemed to be insurmountable adversity.

Principal L.C. Bane
(with Amy Hironaka and Dorothy Harada)

FRANK SATOSHI "JAY" SASAGAWA

Current Residence: Menlo Park, California
Prewar Residence: Palo Alto, California

On December 7th, 1941, I was at the home of the Ishizakis. They are very close family friends. In fact, after the war, they moved in with my parents until they were able to resettle on their own. The day of the attack, all of us were getting haircuts from Mr. Ishizaki and we were shocked when we heard that the Japanese bombed Pearl Harbor. I wasn't frightened at first but did not like the thought of war with Japan—not because I was Japanese, but just the thought of our country involved in a war.

The rumor at that time was that we were going to be evacuated to a place called Manzanar. My parents stated that we were going to drive to camp. My dad sold one of our cars and bought a trailer and my mother made a number of duffel bags in order to pack limited personal belongings that we could throw into the trailer. But that never came to pass. My brother was attending USC at the time and since they had a five-mile limit on travel for *Nikkei*s after the war broke out, he did not feel safe to travel up to Palo Alto alone. He was able to obtain buttons that said, "I am Chinese" and made a number of trips home.

At Topaz, my dad was a cook in the mess hall. He would often bring food back to our room in the barracks so we could reheat and eat together as a family. As time went on, I met friends and found where they ate, and I would eat with them at their block mess hall or they ate at my mess hall.

I went to Topaz High School, but I still had mixed emotions about being in camp and not knowing what the future held for me. I was not a good student but I participated in a lot of sports. I did play basketball, went out for track. I wasn't active in school functions or student government, but I liked to go to all of the dances. The big day of the year at the end of the school term was the mud football game. They flooded an area the size of a football field, and we played mud football against the teachers. We went after teachers that we weren't too fond of and tackled them.

The other funny incident that I remember is that we tipped over a guardhouse similar to a telephone booth, where Japanese old men would be stationed to keep an eye on mischievous kids like us. The guard would chase us shouting epithets, but luckily we didn't get caught. I

Mud Football Game

was a rascal then. I can also recall being picked on by some of the older fellows. I worked in a mess hall for awhile serving food and was working in different block when the Tani brothers—Paul was one of them—made me put on make-up and serve food. It was sort of an initiation, but I didn't like it.

When I reflect back on my life regarding the forced evacuation from the West Coast, I feel that it may not have been as devastating for my peers as it definitely was for our parents and their peers. Their lives were changed overnight. It must have been overwhelming not knowing what the future had in store for them. I do not feel that the reparations from the government were sufficient when you consider the agony, hardship, and suffering they were subjected to. The apology and reparations were much too late for those who were gone before it was approved.

Some of the things that anger me now is when I hear comments that the evacuation was for our own protection. I understand that some of the internees our age say that camp life was lot of fun. It may have been for them, but they should explain the whole picture as to how it affected the whole family, especially their parents. There are still many people in this country who are ignorant about the Japanese American internment camp experience.

DAISY UYEDA SATODA

Current Residence: San Francisco, California
Prewar Residence: Oakland, California

Seiko Akahoshi Brodbeck, Marty Oshima Egan, and I were returning home from the movies on December 7, 1941. We had attended church services earlier in the day at the West Tenth Japanese Methodist Church. Seiko remembers that the theater manager stopped the movie and announced that all military men should return to their base immediately. We passed Nikkaido Stationery Store on Franklin Street and the newspapers on the stand in front, had four-inch high black headlines, screaming, "Japs Bomb Pearl Harbor." We were frightened and started to run. Marty and Seiko wanted to go home, but I wouldn't let them because I was too scared to go home alone as it was already turning dark.

I went to Lincoln School where the student body population was 98% Chinese Americans. The one *hakujin* girl in the class said, "What are you doing here?" I slunk away as no one came to my defense. And she was one girl we all hated. She was cross-eyed and had a big nose that made her sound very nasally. The Chinese girls would always whisper that, "Ethel Simon was a Jew." I didn't know what a Jewish person was. I though she was just plain white and pasty looking. I felt that all the Chinese Americans in my class were secretly happy that this was happening to us as China and Japan had been at war since 1937 and most of their families hated the Japanese. December 8 was a miserable day for me as I lost all of my friends that day. I was happy when we had to leave for camp.

Our Topaz '45 class was lucky; we still had another two years to be kids, to enjoy an almost normal high school, and we were able to make a number of friends through shared experiences and schooling. Our class made the most of it. We were given the opportunity to develop leadership abilities, participate in team sports and varsity squads, become student body and class officers, got to plan and go to dances and proms, work on the yearbook and school newspapers, and join different clubs.

We had wonderful school assemblies. The residents built a high school gymnasium and auditorium. Of course, the duo of Clem [Nakai] and Joker [Hada] performed the most outrageous comedic routines. They were timely, they were funny, they were clever, and they were talented beyond belief. All of these hilarious skits were extemporaneous exhibitions.

Dot Harada Oda, the late Chiyo Date Iino, Florence Nagano Miyashiro, and June Egashira Koba sang in trios or in duets. Marty Oshima Egan and Peggy Shiozawa Wehara taught some gals ballet and they made costumes out of their slips and a long skirt and with props of white pillars, constructed by the stage crew, choreographed a most professional routine to the music of the "Waltz of the Flowers." And we will always remember the appropriately costumed Jim Fujita and Florence Nagano riding a bicycle and singing, "Bicycle Built for Two." And who will ever

Movie Night, Block 9 Mess Hall

forget the multitalented jazz singer, the late Elsie Itashiki Callegari, and her inimitable renditions of "Cow Cow Boogie" and "I Got a Gal in Kalamazoo." Elsie later sang professionally and recorded several albums under her professional name "Teal Joy." These were just a few of the musical talents and productions that entertained the student body. The students, advisors, and stage crews were ingenious and clever in working up routines and making costumes and props.

The school dances were fun. The balls and proms were semiformal, meaning jackets for the boys, and it was mostly for couples. The other dances did not require a date so the stag line was long. You didn't have to know how to dance because it was mostly "slow dancing," which meant you just swayed to the music and took a few steps to turn around in circles. The lights were always turned off with just one light for the disc jockey so he could read the labels on the 78 rpm wax records. Everyone loved the Big Bands—music by Tommy and Jimmy Dorsey, Glenn Miller, Count Basie, Kay Kyser, Benny Goodman, Duke Ellington, and others. Favorite dance tunes were "Till Then," "The Man I Love," One O'clock Jump," "I Can't Get Started," and "Chattanooga Choo Choo." Tubby Yoshida owned a lot of these records. It seemed as if the same people were on the dance committees: decorations, invitations, music, refreshments, and clean up. We used to buy Spackle from the hardware store in Delta to make the concrete floor slippery so we could dance. We decorated the mess hall with streamers of crepe paper.

Graduation from Topaz High in 1945, the last graduating class, was wonderful. We spent three years together, although many of our classmates had already left camp to finish up their schooling on the outside, and now we were ready to face an unknown world. We had a senior banquet, a senior picnic, baccalaureate services, a yearbook. We wore black caps and gowns and most of the girls wore rayon stockings (silk was long gone for use in the war effort, and nylon hose was yet to be invented) and high heels. I was able to go to Salt Lake City with my older sister Doris and I bought a beautiful two-piece black-and-white checkered-sharkskin dress suit which had a sassy peplum. It cost $11 and I thought it was beautiful beyond words. My sister Kaye sent me a pair of black baby-doll ankle-strap sandals with 2½" heels. I felt very grown up. Clem will not remember this, but he took me to the senior prom.

As we enter into the twilight of our years, we can look back on our incarceration as one of the most shameful chapters in the history of the United States. But we have survived and have made the most of our lives. For me, the best part of the internment experience is the wonderful friends and acquaintances I made at the Tanforan Assembly Center in San Bruno, California, and the Topaz, Utah, concentration camp where we were incarcerated from 1942 to 1945. Those three years were both incredibly bad and incredibly good, and it never should have happened. Hopefully, it will never happen again to any other group of people.

Commencement

Exercises

Topaz City High School

Theme
"Leave Then the Dreams of Yesterday
and
Build a Real Tomorrow"

High School Auditorium
June 1, 1945
7:30 p. m.

Graduating Class of June 1945

Abey, Edith
Akita, Wasco
Akiyama, Hajime
Aoyagi, Hatsuye
Aoyagi, Toshiko
Asazawa, Ken
Asoo, Rose
Baba, Isao
Bell, Paul
Date, Chiyo
Doami, Junji
Dowke, Carvin
Egashira, June
Fujii, Dewey
Fujii, Hanako
Fukada, Mary
Fukuhara, Warren
Furusho, Miyeko
Hada, Juji
Hamachi, Roy
Hara, Sadame
Harada, Dorothy
Haramaki, Yoshi
Hatashita, Nobutoshi
Hayashi, Betty
Hideshima, Kazuko
Hironaka, Amy
Hironaka, Mary
Horita, Sakae
Ichisaka, Kiyoto
Ihara, Kimi
Ikeda, Ruby
Ikenoyama, Fred
Inouye, Takara
Ishida, Kumiko
Ito, Tatsuko
Iwaki, Mary
Iwasa, Sus
Iwasaki, Janet
Iwata, Edward
Kaku, Chester
Kawabata, Harry
Kawabata, Toshiro
Kawamoto, Shigeru
Kawamura, Roy

Kawata, Natsuko
Keikoan, Yoshiko
Kenmotsu, Sotoi
Kikuchi, Ernest
Kimura, Joe
Kiyomura, Tatsue
Kobayashi, Ayako
Kobayashi, George
Konno, Kumio
Kumagai, Tomiko
Kumekawa, Ryozo
Kusunoki, Kiyoshi
Marubayashi, Ruri
Maruoka, Kazuo
Masuda, Tommie
Masunaga, Misao
Matsumoto, Mary
Matsunami, Yoshio
Morita, Joe
Nagamoto, Masayoshi
Nagasawa, Emi
Nakagiri, Kikuko
Nakahira, Ritsuko
Nakai, Hirokazu
Nakamoto, Rose
Nakamura, Betty
Nakamura, Henry
Nakamura, James
Nakashige, Mary
Nakata, Akio
Namba, Shizuo
Nihei, Ryo
Noda, Jim
Nodohara, Eugene
Ochi, Somao
Ogata, Yoko
Ogawa, Agnes
Ogo, Kiyoshi
Ohara, Wichi
Okada, Hiro
Okawachi, George
Oku, Kazuye
Okumoto, Fumiko
Ono, Paul
Ota, Hiroshi

Otsuki, Terumi
Oshima, Martha
Ozaki, Tatsuko
Saiki, Fumi
Sanford, Jean
Sanjo, Richard
Sano, Tatsuo
Sasaki, Takeo
Sato, Lena
Sato, Ruby
Shimada, Yosh
Shimamura, Mitsuko
Shimosaka, June
Shiozawa, Peggy
Sonoda, Rey
Sonoda, Yuki
Sumimoto, Masaru
Suzuki, Michio
Takagawa, Leslie
Takahashi, Mary
Takahashi, Jimmy
Takahashi, Toki
Takahashi, William
Takai, Akio
Takaki, Kaoru
Tamura, Teruyo
Tsuchihashi, Yuki
Tsuchiya, Mary
Tsujisaka, Alice
Utsumi, Bob
Uyeda, Daisy
Yamada, Amy
Yamada, Tom
Yamanaka, Henry
Yamasaki, Ichiro
Yamashiro, Richard
Yamate, Herbert
Yanagi, Takehiko
Yanagi, Takeshi
Yoshida, Kiyoko
Yoshifuji, Yaeko
Yoshino, Patty
Yoshiura, Keiko
Yoshiwara, Hiroko

MARY IWAKI SCHULZ

Current Residence: San Rafael, California
Prewar Residence: San Francisco, California

I t is now well over sixty years since those days and my remembrances are very vague. The details of the actual move are very sketchy. I can only recall the general chaos and frantic preparations my parents were involved in with the short notice that was allowed them before the evacuation.

My family lived in the Richmond district on California Street (in the Avenues) where my parents had a dry cleaning and alteration business. Since there were very few Japanese at that time in that general area, all my early friends were Caucasians. I never felt excluded until the war broke out. Then, because of the intensity of the anti-Japanese sentiment, some friends became uncomfortable in pursuing our friendship. However, my teachers at Presidio Junior High School were generally sympathetic and I remember kind notes from classmates were collected and given to me at the time of evacuation.

Santa Anita, the reception center, was a shocker. Our family of five was assigned to a single horse stall which only contained metal cots. I recollect that we were given burlap sacks to fill with hay for bedding.

The incidents that stand out in my memory were the routine inspections of the housing stalls for contraband materials that were conducted by government employees. I remember my mother burying her scissors in the ground and my father destroying pictures that connected him to Japan or to his relatives.

Topaz: Overall I see a picture of desolation, a development placed in an arid, inhospitable area, desert-like, where sandstorms were a common occurrence. There was no protection from the wind that penetrated the interior of the tar-papered barracks and deposited a layer of fine sand in our living quarters. One incident that remains with me is the particularly sad event when an elderly bachelor living in our block who regularly took his dog for walks unwittingly walked too closely to the barbed wire fence. A young, nervous, trigger-happy sentry yelled for him to halt and, when the old man failed to do so quickly, was shot to death. I remember the discussions that ensued following the killing. Where, we asked ourselves, could the victim have gone if he was intent on escaping from the camp? The killing was completely unjustified and there was no recourse. We felt a terrible sense of powerlessness and bitterness.

There were older *Nisei* who shared their many talents with the younger generation. I remember the piano teachers, librarians, sewing teachers, and craft instructors. There were many fine role models in those *Nisei* teachers who taught at the schools alongside the War Relocation Authority teachers brought in from the outside. Despite the makeshift classrooms and inadequate supplies and equipment, the teachers forged ahead and tried their best to instruct sometimes demoralized and angry young teenagers.

The teachers from the outside were generally idealistic and highly motivated individuals. Especially memorable was the high school counselor who encouraged me to continue with my education despite the misgivings of my practical parents who felt that a minority Japanese female should attend sewing or secretarial school. However, Miss Gerard, the counselor, went ahead and processed my application to UC Berkeley. I was accepted and was aided by an initial grant from the American Friends Service Committee. The Friends consistently aided Japanese Americans as they made the transition from camp life to civil society.

"Girl Ask Boy" Dance Bid

ELLEN SETSUKO SHIMADA SHIMASAKI

Current Residence: Hayward, California
Prewar Residence: Sacramento, California

I was only thirteen at the time of Pearl Harbor, so I didn't get the whole significance of the thing. My mother must have gone to church or something and she came home and she was, "Ohhhh!" so excited and was shaking all over. She was very disturbed by the whole thing. She was so afraid that people would come and pick on her, you know. She was afraid for quite a while. I remember the Chinese students; they wore little buttons that said, "I'm Chinese" so that nobody would pick on them. So I guess there was a little bit of that. When they had the fall of Bataan and all those Philippine attacks, it had kind of an impact because some of the Filipinos—I remember in Stockton they have a lot of Filipinos—they shot some Japanese people. My mother was really afraid. Filipino Town was kind of right next to J-Town. So she was really afraid of the Filipinos, too. She was afraid that they might shoot her because she read in the Japanese paper about such incidents in Stockton.

We went to Sacramento Assembly Center. I can't recall how we got there but we were gathered on one street and there were buses that took us to Camp Wallerga. It wasn't the fair grounds; it wasn't a racetrack or anything. It must have been an open, desolate area that they built a camp there. The worst thing about that place was they didn't have flush toilets. It was just a hole-in-the-ground thing. We had to sit next to somebody. Our butts were practically touching. They had a curtain that came down so it hid your face, but it didn't hide the rest of your body. If you made any noises everybody could hear. I felt constipated going there at first, because I didn't want to go or I had to go in the middle of the night when nobody was there.

We were sent to Tule Lake. We were there about a year when they had the "No, no" and all those things. Since my family said, "Yes," we were sent to Topaz. Tule Lake became the segregation center. In Tule Lake the washroom had a long row of noisy galvanized faucets like a horse trough. So when we went to Topaz, we thought, "Wow, white porcelain sinks! Individual ones!" Topaz was nicer than Tule Lake camp. Tule Lake had very hard water. When you washed your hair, it was not very nice. When it rained, we would catch rainwater in buckets so we could wash our hair in softer water. When it snowed, we would just try to get the water from the snow.

Very few friends from Tule came to Topaz. I know Florence Nagano (Miyashiro now) was from Tule Lake and she's also from Sacramento, and Jane Kuroko (who's Jane Kono now). But she lived on the other end of camp. She was a very good friend that I used to chum around with in Sacramento. But when we went to camp, since she was on the other end of camp, I didn't see her very much. I lived in Block 11 and she lived in 40, the very last block.

I liked geometry and chemistry the most. But the only thing was, with the science class like chemistry, we didn't get to do any experiments because all we had was a textbook. When I went to Berkeley, I could barely tell a beaker from a flask because we never had those like the other kids in high school. They knew what to do and I didn't know what to do. We had to catch up. My major was science. I had physiology in Berkeley. For about a year, I worked as a lab tech at UC Hospital. Fred was there. He was a pharmacy student there. At that time they only had a small cafeteria where the workers and the students ate at the same place. That's where I met Fred.

I worked as a nurse's aide in Topaz. I think Kiko [Nakagiri Ishida] was in the barracks right across from us and she was interested in nursing. She was going to work as a nurse's aide, so I guess I went there too because we needed something to do. There was very little training, but there was this lady that was the head nurse—she was kind of an old lady—but she did teach us how to make the patient's bed. I remember how to give bed baths and things like that. She tried to teach us how to give shots. We used to shoot the lemon with the hypodermic needle. So I guess she did teach us.

We gave the patients shots almost right away. I was really shaky and afraid, but the first one I gave was for a man with terminal cancer. When I gave him the shot he said, "Very good, very good," so I was happy. We had to prepare our own morphine solution. We would put a morphine tablet and sterile water in a teaspoon that was soaked in alcohol and hold it over a Bunsen burner and then soak it up into the syringe. I remember one time when I was on the night shift all by myself and this patient with terminal tuberculosis wanted a morphine shot. I guess I didn't drain the spoon very well and I just put it over the burner and PHHEWWT! I thought the whole hospital was going to be on fire! I was so scared; I was really shaky. I just put a towel over it and doused out the flame. I also spoiled one morphine pill. I don't know if they kept very good track of it. So that really scared me.

When I was giving the shot, I was the only one there and I was more or less in charge. The most important shift is in the morning. The evening shift after school is not as busy and not as important. When you think about it, that was a lot of responsibility for a bunch of kids. Right now I'm seventy-four, so at that time I must have been fourteen or fifteen and they entrusted us with something so serious. I don't know how I ever did that. It must have been pretty nervy to do that, but they let us do it. We didn't realize that we were doing something so grave and serious.

I attend the reunions. Now that we're older, we think back about all the unique experiences we had that no one else has had and it makes me feel like going to the reunions more. I talk to Tomi [Kumagai Iwamoto] once in awhile. She lived in the next barracks from me. Kiko [Nakagiri Ishida], I don't see her as often because she lives so far away. But when we get in touch, we are very close.

Graduates Looking Toward the Future

SABURO "SAM" SHIMOMURA

Current Residence: Salt Lake City, Utah
Prewar Residence: San Francisco, California

I heard about the attack on Pearl Harbor, December 7, 1941 as I was leaving church. I went to the Japanese Church of Christ on Post and Octavia Streets. I was a good boy then. I went to church regularly. The minister was Reverend Eiji Kawamorita, father of Emily [Emi] Kawamorita, who was in our class. Her brother was Joe. I was sitting in a car on Bush Street when the war broke out. I just heard that Pearl Harbor was bombed. I said, "What's Pearl Harbor?" I didn't know what was going on. I was a happy kid, easy going.

I went to school on Monday, the day after Pearl Harbor. I remember two guys: Phillip Young, a Chinese American boy, and a Filipino kid named Joaquin Arago. They picked on me pretty bad. They called me names and they wanted to fight. I was a little kid back then, about five feet tall. I didn't say a word. I put my tail between my legs and went on home.

In getting ready to go to camp, we stored most of our household goods in the basement of the house we lived in. As ordered, we checked in our shortwave radio to the FBI, which was located on Buchanan Street, close to Nichibei

Bussan, the store owned by Dave Tatsuno. The FBI threw our radio on top of a lot of other contraband articles which were turned in by the Japanese. My mother had a piano which she had to sell for $5. She had an Easy washing machine and she had to sell that for $5, too.

The train ride from Tanforan to Delta, Utah, was a thirty-nine-hour ride and we had to keep the shades down all the time and there was an MP [military police] armed guard at the front of each car. We sat in straight-back chairs in the coach section in very old trains. Every time a regularly scheduled passenger or freight train came by, they switched us over to a siding.

When we got to the Delta train station, some 6 x 6 trucks picked us up to take us to Topaz. I could not believe the dust when we got there. We stood up all the way in the truck—and that included my mom and my grandmother, Natsu Shimomura, who was 87 years old. She died in 1949 when she was 94 years old. She was my father's mother. She came to America when Dad went back to Japan to pick her and my mom up. My grandma stayed at home; she did not work. She survived it all. She was the greatest. I really loved that old lady.

I cut my finger off when I was in high school. I did it in woodshop. Dave Yamate was in that class. He was an upper classman. Our classmate Tom Masuda [Beau Jack] was in that class, too. My finger got ground up like hamburger because it went through a joiner plane. I was planing a 1"x 6" piece of wood which was vertical. As I was planing it, my thumb flipped off the wood right above the blade. There was a straight line of blood all the way across the ceiling. I was numb and in shock. The only thing I remember was Tom Masuda saying, "Hey, do you want me to knock you out so you won't feel the pain?" He was serious because he was an amateur boxer back then. Someone called the ambulance and they took me to the hospital.

I ground up the ring finger on my left hand. I started to feel the pain after I got to the hospital because I guess I was in shock until that time. There was a Dr. [John] Teshima and also a Dr. [James] Goto, the head surgeon. Dr. Teshima operated on me and he really messed my finger up because the nerve was right beneath my skin and every time I touched anything, the pain was so bad you would not believe it. After I went into the Army, I checked into the hospital in 1946 and they operated on that finger again and they fixed it up. Dr. Goto didn't operate on me because I never complained about it.

I stayed out of school for less than a week. I was very self-conscious about my finger. I said that I was quitting school and not going back because of the missing finger. I was thinking of an excuse not to return to school. This was just before Christmas and I was ready to quit school when one of my teachers came to the hospital to visit me and she said, "You can't quit school." She brought me a pair of gloves. I don't even remember her name. She was Caucasian. That was so nice of her. She said, "I don't want you to be embarrassed with your missing finger, so you can wear these gloves when you come back to school."

There was a Frank Shidawara who blew off some fingers on one hand in a firecracker accident before the war, and he was very self-conscious and always hid that one hand in his pocket. He was a mean guy. He used to come looking for me and chase me all over camp whenever he saw me. I don't know why, but for some reason he hated me. He was crazy. He was very strong with his one good arm. He would put the shovel under his armpit and pick up a load of dirt with that one arm and flip it over. He was tough. No one wanted to mess with him. I understand he ended up in San Quentin for shooting some *Nisei* guy. Whatever happened to him? Actually I was happy to hear he went to San Quentin and I was sorry that he got out. I was so scared of that guy.

In Topaz I used to smoke with Dave Yamate. He and I worked at the hospital together. We drove the ambulance together. That was after I lost my finger. No, I did not have a driver's license. I worked as a driver because I wanted to pay back because I was so grateful for the ambulance that took me to the hospital when I ground up my finger.

On one of our ambulance runs I remember this guy, this Mr. Hanamura, who was also from San Francisco. He went out fishing one night outside of the camp and he got back about nine or ten o'clock at night, and he got hit by a semi truck. I went to pick him up with Dave and every bone in his body was broken and I had to go tell his wife that he had died. He had a son named Nobuhisa who returned to San Francisco after the war.

We used to pick up and take home the nurses who worked on the night shift. Do you remember that Dr. Collier that came down from Salt Lake City and operated on several people who became blind after the operation? Several surgeries failed, so the whole ambulance crew went on strike.

I didn't graduate from Topaz High. My family left Utah in November of 1944, right after I started my senior year because my dad got a job in Ogden. My brother Ken was either still at Michigan State or he was in the service, so he was not living with us. I stayed there until April of 1946. I went to school for a little while but I just couldn't adjust to the outside world. The war ended in August of 1945 and, boy, I tell you, those high school boys came chasing after us and wanted to beat the hell out of us in Ogden. I quit school before then anyway because I just couldn't adjust. I was hanging around at home, the pool halls, wherever.

Sewer Pipe Repairs - Topaz

HIROKO YOSHIWARA SUDA

Current Residence: Oakland, California
Prewar Residence: Oakland, California

No one was arrested after December 7th. I was really shocked. We were at a family picnic at Lake Merritt. There was a car that went by with kids in it yelling "Japs!" That was the first time. Everybody in the neighborhood was pretty nice to us. After war was declared, we had to obey civil defense orders. I don't remember what time the curfew was and all that. We pulled the shades down for a black-out when an alarm went off. Then I think when the alarm goes off again, that's when you could pull your shades back up.

After the evacuation orders came, we just put everything in the garage. Our parents thought that we would be gone for only about three months or so. It was really done so fast they left everything: Furniture in the house, washing machine, bedding. We could take only what we could carry to camp, so we just thought it was for a few months. We weren't really prepared.

The train to Topaz was such a dirty, dusty car, I mean, train. Every time we came to a station, we had to put down the shades and all. It was more like a prison. At Topaz, all the people had dust masks on. "Gee, what kind of place

This Note Given to Hiroko at Time of Evacuation

At this time of your departure from Oakland we wish to express our friendship for you and our belief in you as neighbors and fellow Americans. We are disturbed, as you are, by any implication that evacuation reflects in some way against your loyalty and integrity. We who know you best have complete confidence in your devotion to the democratic ideals for which America stands.

We recognize how serious is this dislocation of your lives. In addition to sharing the hardships of war equally with the rest of us this new burden is forced upon you which we do not have to bear. We apologize for any discourtesy which any of our fellow citizens have shown you, for it is rooted in un-American racism or caused by an emotional hysteria which generally arises in war time. However, we believe the officials who have been entrusted with the supervision of the evacuation are concerned about your welfare and will be as helpful as possible.

We pledge ourselves to do everything we can to reduce the hazards and soften the effects of exile. We promise that we will work to the end that after the war is over you and your children shall share in all the freedom which we expect for ourselves.

Please avail yourselves of the services offered by the women of the churches of Oakland on evacuation day. They will consider it a privilege to help you in any way.

Our prayers and goodwill go with you in this new experience. In a happier day we shall welcome you cordially as friends and neighbors if you choose to return to your homes in Oakland.

Those of us whose names are signed to this statement do not speak officially for our organizations, for these organizations have not had opportunity to meet, but we are confident that this simple gesture of friendship is representative of the vast majority of the Christians of this city. We invite you to write to us so that we can keep track of you. We want you to feel free to ask us for any aid which we can render.

May the Lord bless you and keep you—on your going out and on your coming home.

Mrs. Joseph A. Woods
Pres. of Oakland Council of Church Women
52 Sharon Avenue, Piedmont

Lawton Harris
Executive Sec. East Bay Church Federation
Y. M. C. A. Building, Oakland

Robert Inglis
Pres. East Bay Ministers' Fellowship
3805 Piedmont Avenue, Oakland

Kumi Ishida

did we come to?" All this dust flying around because they didn't have any gravel or anything. Like a dust storm. And that place could get so hot and so cold. I'm glad they issued the pea coats. That really helped.

I don't know whether we had a choice, but everybody had these flannel shirts, plaid shirts. I noticed the boys had turned theirs inside out to make it a different pattern. I thought it was kind of interesting because otherwise, everyone's wearing the same thing. Later on, people had different catalogs like Spiegel's, so some styles were a little different.

I didn't like school at all because when we first got there we were sitting on almost like picnic benches and a table. And then you'd have this pot-bellied stove. And when it was cold, it was hot. I mean, if you're real close to it you're hot because they were burning coal to keep warm. I didn't feel like school. I didn't feel like studying at all. So I just took up space. I didn't have any strong feelings about the teachers. I guess they were doing their best. I enjoyed Mr. Dave Tatsuno. But I don't remember what the name of the class or what kind of class it was. I think I just enjoyed listening to him. He was kind of like a philosopher or something. But other than that, school was just...I didn't learn anything. I really didn't apply myself. I'm really ashamed of it because I should have gotten something out of it, three years of being there.

Mr. Mas Yabuki had gone out of his way to fix up his classroom. His classroom was made into a little room where he had his office and then room for the kids. He had a candy jar and he'd pass it around. I used to enjoy that, too. He taught art. I enjoyed it because it was a little different atmosphere. But one day he was really upset. He was just about in tears. The kids had broken into the classroom and did something to it. They vandalized his office a little. I think they might have even taken the candy jar. It was too bad. He was trying so hard to do the best teaching.

Mr. Ostlund was very hard of hearing and he would ask us to make an oral presentation of some sort, a book report or something. And some of the boys would get up and just mouth what they were going to say. Mr. Ostlund, being hard of hearing, he just thought they were speaking and he'd clap and say how wonderful when the lesson was finished. And everybody else was laughing because they didn't say a word. They just mouthed what they were saying. It was funny to us, but I felt kind of bad about that. I felt so sorry for him. I think it was an English class.

You wonder what kind of students would think of that. Oh, dear. I guess boys will be boys.

I worked at the Topaz Hospital as a nurse's aide, but I didn't have regular training. I thought there was a class or something. But I didn't get any training, just learning by working. We learned how to make morphine using a Bunsen burner and then using a tablespoon of solution (water) and then heating it up and then adding the morphine to dissolve it. I remember the head nurse—I don't know what her name was. She was Japanese and she told me when the doctors come in to look at the patients, you're supposed to follow him. But when you come to a door, you're supposed to go in front of him and open the door for him. I thought, "Gee, I hope it's not being disrespectful to all of a sudden run in front of the doctor to do that.'"

I remember that one of the *hakujin* registered nurses was from the South and frequently spoke of eating fried bananas. One night, on the night shift of the men's ward, she made a skillet of fried bananas for us. It was a treat, a little different from the usual mess hall food.

I started—I think—on the night shift. I'm not really sure if it was 12:00 AM to 8:00 AM or something like 12:00 AM to 6:00 AM. I started in the men's ward. There was somebody—a young fellow that was a patient for some time—who seemed awfully popular. I don't know what kind of illness he had, but I know he was a long time in the hospital. He seemed to be writing to Jane Wyman and he had a letter that he'd received from her. She had said that "Ronnie" was home or something. Or that "Ronnie" was away or something like that— Ronald Reagan. She said that he was concerned about the Japanese being put in camp and he wanted to know what his experiences were.

I hope the internment doesn't happen again to anybody else. After all, it's a lot of time being locked up. And we're American citizens, which doesn't seem right. And we didn't have any choice. We were told we had to do this. At the beginning, I thought I didn't want reparations. But after really thinking it over, our freedom was taken away all that time. And it was a long time. It should have been the best years of lives, those three years of high school. I thought it was appropriate that they give us something, when you think about the little children who were born there or were only a few years old.

MASARU "WACKY" SUMIMOTO

Current Residence: Berkeley, California
Prewar Residence: Oakland, California

There were seven or eight of us at my house and we knew were gonna have to go to camp. And we said, "'Hey, let's give everybody a name.'" We were looking at a comic book and there was a character named "Wacky." A guy said, "'Hey, that's a perfect name for you.'" Everybody lost their nick-name later, but mine stuck. Old, old friends call me "Mas." But I don't mind being called "Wacky." A lotta guys, after they got out of camp, they got a different "American" name and put it in front, like "Charles."

My father was a wholesale liquor and wine distributor before camp. He made a very good living. I never went hungry. I think I had it a better than a lot of Japanese people did. He owned that business. My older brother told me stories. You know those mom-and-pop grocery stores all over the Bay Area? I betcha every one of them owed my dad money. But my dad never collected. He was the worst businessman you ever wanted to...until my brother started taking over and they started getting a little bit better. He would go to customers and sit there and booze all day long. How you gonna make any money that way? But that's how close the community was, see?

As a result of being sent to camp, my dad lost the business. After the war, he became a maintenance man at a hotel. He didn't know anything about that kind of work. It's amazing. Maybe all the guys that *he* owed money to never did collect. Maybe losing the business got him out of the hole, I don't know. In those days, it was all bribery. You got away with more stuff. My dad would get by with more stuff by giving a cop a case of beer. That's the way it was.

My dad was an alcoholic, so he had to sweat it out in camp. But then he started a brewery in camp for his own use. He could drink up a storm, boy. It was so funny, because when you ferment rice, it smells. He had glass tubes going all over. One of the rooms was empty and he scrounged around and found barrels and he fermented the rice. He knew how to do that. I guess when they threw the rice out at the mess halls, he got it. Lotta guys had connections: My cousin was able to go to Salt Lake and every time he'd come back, he'd bring the old man a fifth.

Do you know about the prostitutes in camp? Nobody ever told you about the prostitutes in camps, huh? But I don't wanna go into that. There was girls when we first went to Tanforan, I remember. I was a young kid then, of course. Somebody said, "Hey, there's a couple of prostitutes down there in the stable area.'" "Texas Mary" and "Battleship." What do I know about prostitution in camp? I was just a kid. But, somebody told me, "'Hey, there's a coupla whores down there.'" That's all *I* know. I think they were *Kibei*-ish girls, but one had to be from Texas.

There was gangs, but not vicious gangs. Not vicious. Groups. They hung around together. There was naturally the San Francisco bunch that stuck around together. And Oakland guys. Neighborhood guys, you know. There's a little clique, you know, all over. But the camp life I saw brought everybody together. I probably would have never met the Palo Alto guys, Oakland, and Washington. They came in from Sacramento, too. They all mingled together. It was very good. It just brought our generation of Japanese that much closer together. Really. I mean, you couldn't help but get closer together, you had no place to go.

There was times when it was uncomfortable, but up to a point. Well, there *was* a conflict between Japan-born guys and American-born. *Kibei*s and *Nisei*s. There was always that conflict. My oldest brother was a *Kibei*. My other brother was just like me. I know that the *Kibei* guys had a group. And naturally they're against Americans. They're fighting their country. What's the *Nisei* supposed to do, though? He's got Japanese parents, just like *Kibei*. What are they supposed to do? That was the only real serious-type conflict that I saw. Not a whole lotta *Kibei* guys went to join the 442, I'll guarantee you that.

So as far as conflict, there were a few outbreaks between the Oakland and maybe the San Francisco guys, you know, like that. But nothing serious. This group, it was very mild, controlled. They're not a vicious type. I think about the only vicious guys in camp was *our* kids. Nobody fooled with that group. Nobody fooled with the West Oakland guys.

When it came to school, I never missed a day. You had nothing else to do but go to school. It was fun to go to school because they had other activities. I was the worst student in school. I just didn't want to study. I wasn't forced to study. My mom and pop didn't force me to study. My older brother Tut [Tsutomu] is the one who called the shots, like a parent. To this day, he's the man.

I don't know what it would be like if I didn't go to camp. Nobody knows. Fifteen years old, you don't care how cold it is. I never had a bed by myself until I got into camp. At fifteen years old, I don't think you don't really know what hardship is. Your parents know, but I can't tell you what they felt. We barely conversed. They never complained to me. No use complaining to me, I can't do anything for them. We didn't know hardship, for Chrissakes. We were little kids. We're young guys. What's hardship?

Camp life was miserable for a lotta people. I'm sure it was. But if you don't know what "good" is, how do you know you're having it "bad"? Hey, I had cardboard in my shoe before we went into camp, you know? The shoe wore out, you put cardboard in it. That's the way it went. Can you imagine the people who came in from the farms? They had to bust their buns day in and day out. Even the little kids. When they went to camp, there's no more of that stuff. That's was what my wife told me. Her family had a truck farm. My mother never had to make mayonnaise. She never had to make ketchup. I understand the country people all had to make their own stuff. So those people go to camp, it's a different opportunity for them. I know it's wrong that we were in camp. I'll say it's wrong. On the other hand, I made lifelong friends that I probably would never have the opportunity to meet.

HIDETOSHI TAKAHASHI

Current Residence: San Jose, California
Prewar Residence: Oakland, California

On December 7, 1941, I was busy folding papers getting ready for my paper route when I heard on the radio that the Japanese bombed Pearl Harbor. I delivered the papers and returned home to listen to the radio. I was dumbfounded, but not scared. But I was not completely surprised. My brother was going to dental school in San Francisco at that time and I would often ride across the San Francisco Bay Bridge with him because I was having dental work being done at the dental school. As we crossed the bridge, we could see freighters with Japanese flags blowing in the breeze and we would wonder why there were so many. Since I delivered the paper, I would read the headlines every day and followed the news with the ambassadors coming over and the anti-Japanese sentiment in the country, I knew that something was brewing.

My father talked with some pride about Japan going into Manchuria and Korea. I think there was a lot of pride in the Japanese community of the conquests that Japan was making. The principal at Wanto Gakuen talked about this often and he came right out and said he wanted to be the governor of Singapore. Several days later he was picked up by the FBI and was off to some detention camp. The day after December 7th, all classes at Wanto Gakuen stopped. The buses had Wanto Gakuen and some Japanese characters painted on the side. With the closure, all our social interaction with other Japanese kids stopped because that was where we met every day after regular school.

The school was a hot, uncomfortable environment not conducive to learning. We sat on benches with no backs. It was not a pleasant experience. Some of the teachers were weird. Some were nice. I recall one teacher named Ostlund, who was deaf. I thought it was strange to have a deaf person teaching. I remember Miss Matzkin. I heard that she married the governor of Pennsylvania. She must have had some good contacts. There was a Mrs. Nail. Her husband was Lt. Nail, who was in charge of the military police responsible for guarding Topaz camp. She taught French. Well, she was half smashed all of the time. We knew because as soon as you walked into her room, you could smell alcohol.

There were some Japanese teachers that I still remember: Norman Hirose who was a few years older and had graduated in the first class at Topaz. He was smart and taught German and chemistry. Eiko Hosoi taught math. She was a nice-looking gal and we used to make her blush. Then there was Dave Tatsuno. Once you start talking to him you might as well pull up a chair and sit. He likes to talk. Once he told me about a buying trip for the Topaz co-op. The manufacturer would try to pawn off all of the odd sizes on him and they were much too large for the average Japanese. He had no problem getting film for himself and he took a lot of pictures in camp.

I recall the movies where we sat on the floor on blankets and it was stifling hot. I remember when a couple of young kids from our block—San Francisco kids of grammar school age—saw these wide-open spaces and they just walked out of camp to look for scorpions and stones, and they walked and walked and walked. They were finally spotted by the MPs, and they were brought back in a jeep to camp and dumped unceremoniously in the middle of our block. I thought it was funny at that time.

CHIURA OBATA

| Soph Hop May 26 | RAM-BLER | Senior Ball May 30 |

Vol. V No. 8   Topaz City High School   FRIDAY, MAY 25, 1945

Seniors To Graduate June 1

May Day Festival Enjoyed

Although bad weather prevailed on Thursday, the May Day Festival was held with some alterations, Friday, May 11. The original plans were revised, with classes being held in the morning.

The opening ceremony was presented at the platform near the Industrial Arts building. The program consisted of a flag ceremony by the local Boy Scouts and Kaz Maruoka, bugler, an introductory speech by Student Body President Ryozo Kumekawa, and a singspiration conducted by yell leader Clem Nakai.

Following the beginning ceremony, a boys' tug o' war contest between the combined seventh and eighth grade boys against the freshmen occurred. This contest was shortly discontinued because of a faulty rope.

A flashing array of hats distinguished the girls drill team which Paul Bell, was always hard at work marched to the tune of "Stars and stripes Forever." The first place award went to the second period girls.

Seniors Cop Mud Brawl

"Ramblings" Staff Reaches Culmination Of Labor

Representing the work of one of the busiest and most diligent staffs in the history of Topaz journalism is this year's annual. At the editor-in-chief desk is our own student body president, Ryozo Kumekawa. Under him are the able hardworking staffs with their editors and co-editors.

The technical staff, headed by Chester Kaku, consists of Michio Suzuki and Ben Nakahira. A very consistent staff, this group of technicians labored hard and late hours to assemble this year's book.

On this year's literary staff are Sadame Hara, Betty Hayashi, and Dorothy Harada. This small group faced the task of completing the literary sections throughout the journal.

This year's business staff, headed by co-chairmen Tubby Yoshida and Paul Bell, was always hard at work raising the necessary funds for the publication. They directed the Spring Carnival and also sponsored many movies for the public. Others on the staff are Shiz Namba, Harry Inatura.

Senior Enjoy Active Days Prior To Graduation

Climaxing the school year, the last few weeks are the most exciting for those who are to be graduated, for they are promised to be full of activities.

Senior Control Day, May 15, started the ball rolling with the Senior Class President, Junji Doami, acting as principal of Topaz High and the Seniors taking control of the school. Almost every student took the place of a faculty member and the day was acclaimed a huge success.

Next came the Senior Sneak on May 17, which was a surprise even to the seniors. The afternoon was spent at Rec. 34, exchanging calling cards and signing the memory books which accompanied the cards. Refreshments were served and a jam session was held.

With versatile Clem Nakai in charge, Seniors will Tuesday present their long awaited assembly. Mickey Suzuki, vice president of the Student Body, will be the MC and the program will be of a skit nature.

136 Students To Receive Diplomas

After three years of hard, studious labor, one hundred thirty-six seniors will graduate from Topaz High School on June 1, at 7:30 p. m., in the auditorium. Dr. Arthur L. Beeley of the University of Utah will deliver the commencement message to the graduates.

The program is as follows:

Processional .... Class of June,1945

Pledge of Allegiance........
    .... Led by President Junji Doami

National Anthem ....
    .... Graduates and Audience

Invocation.... Reverend Norio Ozaki

Address of Welcome........
    .... President Junji Doami

Violin Selection .... Hatsuye Aoyagi

Theme:
"Leave Them the Dreams of Yesterday and Build a Real Tomorrow"
    Mary Iwaki
    Ryozo Kumekawa

Vocal solo .... Dorothy Harada
    Accompanied by Mrs. Roscoe Bell

Presentation of Diplomas........
    Principal Laverne Bane

Superintendent La Grande Noble

Felicitations to Students........
    Project Director L. J. Hoffman

stripes Forever. The first place award went to the second period girls.

Seniors Cop Mud Brawl

Continuing in aggressiveness throughout the late midafternoon the seniors eked out a win over an overwhelming aggregation of lower classmen in an all out mud brawl held as the main event of the May Day Festival.

With the aid of alumni Tom Tonioka, Ossie Tamaki, Ky Tanamachi, Harlem Sano, and Frank Sasagawa, the elderly seniors made the lower classmen behave.

Making every use of their her-

(Continued on page 2)

raising the necessary funds for the publication. They directed the Spring Carnival and also sponsored many movies for the public. Others on the staff are Shiz Namba, Harry Kawabata, Daisy Uyeda, and Hana Sonoda.

On the sports staff are co-editors Haruru Kojimoto and Richard Yamashro. Without the assistance of the required staff members, these sports editors did their work well.

The girls' sport staff headed by Amy Zamada, was ably assister by Setsuko Asano and Kiko Nakagiri.

Because of the untiring labor done by the whole staff, the year book is tentatively scheduled to be released on either May 28 or 29.

sent their long awaited assembly. Mickey Suzuki, vice president of the Student Body, will be the MC and the program will be of a skit nature.

On Sunday, May 27, the traditional Baccalaureate Services will be held in the civic auditorium.

The program is as follows:

Chairman .... Dr. L. C. Bane
Processional .... Seniors
Prelude .... Mrs. Wallace Crane
Call to Worship ...... Dr. L. C. Bane
Invocation .... Father Stoecke
Hymn ... Now in the Days of Youth
Sermon .... Reverend Motoyoshi
Vocal solo .... June Egashira
Hymn .... I Would Be True
Sermon .... Reverend Shimada
Hymn ... Hear, Hear, O Ye Nations
Benediction .... Reverend Imai

The following evening, May 28, the Senior Banquet will be given in Dining Hall 10 at 7:30, and tickets for reserved seats of the Commencement will be distributed.

Next on the list of activities comes the Senior Ball, May 30; Shizuo Namba headed all committees.

For May 31, the Senior Outing is scheduled and on the last and biggest day of all, June 1, come the Commencement Exercises.

Sophomore Hop Scheduled Saturday

On May 26, 1945, the Sophomores will hold their annual Soohomore Hop with the theme "Moonglow". The place will be Dining Hall 32.

Heading the refreshment committee is Mary Mayeda. Records, George Shimada; Decorations, Tosh Sano; Advertisment, Asako Narahara; Tickets and Bids, Amy Doi and Kaneo Ito.

Principal LaVerne Bane
Superintendent La Grande Noble
Felicitations to Students........
Project Director L. J. Hoffman
Message to Graduates........
.... Dr. Arthur L. Beeley

Class Hymn
"Farewell Topaz High".. Graduates
Recessional........
.... Graduates of June, 1945

Nishimura Receives Scholarship at Harvard

We have just been notified that Dwight Nishimura, who left here last spring for New York City, has been given a scholarship to Harvard University.

While he was here, his scholastic standing ranked close to the top, while he kept himself busy with a wide variety of activities.

Since his relocation Dwight has also done very well. He has led as number one student in most of his classes and very high in the rest of them.

The Topaz High School is very proud of its former students, such as Dwight, who have done so much toward making a better name for the niseis on the outside.

Results of Clean Up Day Essay Contest

In the recent clean-up campaign an essay contest was staged in the high school. Winner of first pdace prize was Isao Shimamura; second, Shig Omori; third, Tommy Nihei. The winning essay is printed on page two.

The following pupils in the elementary schools were awarded prizes in the clean-up poster con-

(Continued on page 2, col.1)

Presenting the Rally Committee . . .

FRONT ROW, left to right: Ray Sonoda, Clem Nakai, Butch Nagasawa, Sakae Horita, Sei Hirose. Back row: Ray Iwata, Chuck Yamasaki, Tatsuo Sano, Junji Doami, Joker Hada, Bob Utsumi.

MARY MATSUMOTO TAKEDA

Current Residence: San Jose, California
Prewar Residence: Berkeley, California

We had to get rid of our belongings for the evacuation. We had a nice piano and we sold it for five dollars. A lady used to come all the way from Alameda to give lessons to my sisters and me. We enjoyed it so much and to think that we sold it for five dollars! We were all heartbroken. We had cameras, which my mother threw away. My parents were more frightened than we were. We even had a gun that we threw away.

We were in Block 5 at Topaz. The Sano family lived across from us. They had a large family with lots of boys. Amy and Mary Tamaki lived in that block and there was Jo Jo and Toa Momii. Toa was something else. His parents had passed away, so he took care of the rest of the family. He did all of the washing. He was quite a guy.

We went to school in those heavy Mackinaws that were too big. Dave Tatsuno has movies of us in those Mackinaws. He was our speech teacher at school and he had access to a camera. There was that blonde girl in our class, almost like an albino. There were a lot of scholars in our class. They were all Japanese, you know, and they all do well in school. There was that *hakujin* girl, too—Jean Sanford.

There was one activity I enjoyed. Eddie Iino led a choir and a lot of my friends like Daisy Uyeda were in it. We used to practice a lot and one Christmas we all got in the back of a big truck and went to Delta to sing Christmas carols at a school. I took tailoring from Mr. Kusunoki. He was nice. I don't know where we got the material from, but we used to make things. I made a coat and when I couldn't do a particular part, I would ask Mr. Kusunoki and he would show me how.

TATSUO TANAKA

Current Residence: Gardena, California
Prewar Residence: Alvarado, California

I was born in Decoto, California, on November 13, 1927. In case you are not familiar with Decoto, it is presently known as Union City. Some of the classmates I knew are Carvin Dowke, Jim Nakamura, Teruo Tsutsui, and Tommy Masuda. When I was one year old, I was diagnosed as having polio. I spent a lot of my infancy in the hospital. I wasn't able to walk until I was four years old.

When the war broke out, my father [Yoshichiro Tanaka] was farming for D.P. Garin Co. in Alvarado, California. Our family was living in Alvarado and, when evacuation orders came, our understanding was we would be taken somewhere for ninety days and then return. We left everything there and left with only with what we could carry.

I never graduated high school. I went to Topaz High through September of 1943 and then went to Tule Lake with my family. While we were in Topaz, my mother [Kikuno Miyama Tanaka] received a telegram from Japan, inviting her to come back to Fukuoka to celebrate her father's 88th birthday [*Bei-ju*]. My mother was determined to go. We left Topaz in September of 1943 for Tule Lake Detention Camp.

In Topaz, I enjoyed meeting new friends there. Living in the country where neighbors are far apart, I didn't have many friends my own age.

From Tule Lake, we went to Japan on a troop transport from Portland, Oregon (via Columbia River) in December 1945. After the war, I worked for the US Army while I was in Japan, first as a foreign national and then as a civilian. I worked for the Department of the Army for twenty-four years in Japan. I retired and returned to the United States in 1984. I regained my US citizenship in 1951. My only regret of the war is that I lost an opportunity for higher learning.

YAEKO YOSHIFUJI TONDO

Current Residence: San Francisco, California
Prewar Residence: Pescadero, California

My name is Yaeko Yoshifuji Tondo. I was born in Pescadero, California, on July 4, 1926. I am the eighth child of my family and that is why the first character in my name is "8—hachi or *ya* in Japanese. My parents were Yutaka Yoshifuji and Chiye Shintaku. They are both from Hiroshima Prefecture. My father came to the US when he was sixteen years old and my mother joined him years later. She was a picture bride.

It was a hard life for my parents and my siblings when we lived on our farm in Pescadero before World War II. Although we had a big house that my father built himself, it was always a struggle to make ends meet. We did not have any luxuries. My mother sewed all of our clothes, made all of our food (ranging from *tofu* to apple pie), and all I can remember from my childhood days was receiving hand-me-downs from my two older sisters.

I don't remember how I heard that we had to leave our home after the Executive Order was issued. I don't remember any signs posted where we lived. We usually received our news about important events from the one and only Japanese market in town. I guess they were the ones who informed us what was going on and that we had to leave.

I really did not have too much to pack since we did not own many material goods. I know that packing was a hard decision for my parents as they had many tools that cost them a great deal of money and were worried about the crop that was ready to harvest.

We always left these decisions up to my mother, which is kind of amazing since she spoke very little English and was not afforded the opportunity in Hiroshima to attend school past primary school.

I remember Tanforan. This was the first place they brought us to. This was a racetrack. I especially remember looking outside of the grandstand behind the barbed-wire fence they had around the entire racetrack to keep us inside. I remember seeing El Camino Real past the barbed wire and watching all of the cars pass us by. I would dream about me being outside the fence and what it was like to be free. I'd give anything to be free, I used to say. I'd give anything to go somewhere, but I was trapped in that place.

I was puzzled as to why we were forced to be cooped up. No one sees us in the sticks so why did we have to leave? I was scared when I saw the guards surrounding us who had guns. I wondered why we were being put in a jail but we all made the most of it. Everything was new to us since our family did not travel very much before the war.

I remember that we had to show our identification cards and that there were rumors that someone was going to poison the water because they considered Japanese dangerous. The food in camps was bad. I remember the slimy lettuce we were served, as the administration would trade the good stuff for money. It was a hard time for all of us.

This was also the first time that I rode on a train. We had to ride the train to Topaz. I remember that there was some type of food scandal there, but I don't remember the details.

We didn't eat together much with our family in camp. My mother and father worked in the mess hall and I started meeting other people living on our block. My brother was in the first twelve *Niseis* to be drafted in Topaz. My other sister Mineko had to transfer to Tule Lake because her husband voted "No-No." My other sister Sayoko went to Cleveland to work. We all had to split up for the first time.

I think it was really hard on us after we were forced out of camp. We had no home to go back to. We had no support and no place to stay.

Looking back on the camp period, I never understood why we had to go. We were good citizens. We were law abiding and did everything we were told to do. How much more did they want to push us?

I now live in San Francisco and have been married to Joe Tondo for over fifty years. We have two children and four grandchildren. I still attend the Topaz Class reunions as often as possible and enjoy talking with everyone.

The recollections expressed in *Blossoms in the Desert* display the strong and determined spirit of an American high school class who was forced to learn and grow in a barbed-wire compound armed with US guards.

Each story presents an undiscovered aspect of life during the challenging war years as well as how the vision and strength of this unique and unified group of individuals have cherished the value of friendship to guide and shape their lives over the past six decades.

BOB UTSUMI

Current Residence: Oakland, California
Prewar Residence: Oakland, California

When I was about thirteen and walking along the street in Oakland, a sailor grabbed by arm and asked, "Are you a Jap?" I answered "No" and broke away and ran like hell. On December 7th, I was in the Roxy Theater. Walking home I heard the newspaper boys yelling, "Extra, extra, Japs bomb Pearl Harbor." I didn't know where Pearl Harbor was, but I felt shame, betrayal, and fear. During one of the first blackouts, someone threw a billiard ball through the plate glass window of my father's photography studio.

The evacuation was an adventure for me. I was in the Boy Scouts, so I liked to pack and helped out as much as I could. We stored all the family goods at the Oakland Methodist Episcopal Church. That turned out to be a good move because we had one *hakujin* member named Lee Mullis who got the camera for Dave Tatsuno. He and his father were members of the OME Church and watched over everything.

At Topaz, Mom worked as a waitress in the mess hall. For the evening meal, she would bring food home and reheat it on a hot plate that she got from Montgomery Ward and doctored up. It was the one meal that we ate together.

Those "home-cooked" meals might have been tied in with shipments of Kikkoman *shoyu* that came in big wooden tubs. Everyone went to the gym with a container and got a share. That was a big treat.

I occupied my time with school. I don't know how I did it, but I graduated and had fairly good grades. We had some terrible teachers. The only good teachers that we had were our campmates. Rosie Watanabe for geometry. Sugihara taught Spanish. Anderson taught chemistry. That guy was dangerous. Dorsey Kobayashi, Chuck Yamazaki, Gus Sonoda, Tats Sano, and the smart girls Dorothy Harada, and Marty Oshima were in that class. As an experiment, Anderson had a large vat of water on the podium and a can of sodium. He demonstrated the making of hydrogen gas by putting a little of the sodium into the water and making it fizz. Chuck, Gus, and I were in the back of the room and yelled out, "More." So Anderson added a larger chunk of sodium and it really fizzes and pops. We kept urging "More." He took a big chunk of sodium and dropped it into the glass vat and, pow, it explodes! The first three rows got wet. We were just howling with laughter. Only after I related the story to Paul Bell did I realize the gravity of the situation: What was created in the vat was sodium hydroxide.

When my kids hear about the nicknames that we had for each other they just laugh: Wacky, Tubby, Beaver, Bubbles, Chinky, Blacky, Black Boy, C. J. And some of the expressions: "No sweat, no *shimpai*." When the Hawaiians came, they introduced a few: "Buddaheads," "kotonks."

I finished high school in June 1945 when I was sixteen years old. I joined my uncle and his family who had returned to Warm Springs, California. They brought everything they had including some young celery plants they had grown in Utah. They kept them under blankets to keep them from freezing when they crossed the Sierra. When they stopped for the night, they brought the plants into the motel room. Somehow they got their plants through the agricultural checkpoint at the California border and that's how they started their first crop.

JUNIOR SOCIAL COMMITTEE

GLORIA YASUNAKA YAMAUCHI

Current Residence: San Mateo, California
Prewar Residence: Volcano, Hawaii

I was born in Mountain View, Hawaii, on January 21, 1928. On December 7, my brother and I were coming home from town. On the way home we stopped at a gas station to fill up the gas and we heard about it. It didn't penetrate our mind, this unbelievable thing. We were on the Big Island and far enough away that it didn't penetrate our minds.

My father was taken in and interned. First in Hawaii, and then he was sent on to Honolulu to Sand Island. That's where they interned a lot of the Japanese. They even interned the politicians of Hawaii! Like Senator Abe, Congressman Sakagihara. They were all interned. They were government politicians and they were right there with my father.

There were other families that were brought over to the mainland. The reason my mother came was that if the family came with her, like the spouse came with the husband and the children, the family would be together. But if the wives didn't want to come and remained in Hawaii, then they would be separated and the husbands would be sent off to another internment camp. There was no special reason we went to Topaz. We went there because my father was sent there. We came over on a boat, an Army transport boat.

We really were not prepared for the weather at Topaz. We had overcoats, but they weren't heavy enough. They issued some GI-issued things, so a lot of the bachelors were walking around with those big, big Army overcoats and things. I guess we really weren't prepared. In Hawaii, we wore sandals and things like that, and of course we came over with shoes. The people were very curious at school—because we were pretty dark and the clothing we wore. I would say we wore pretty colorful clothes. Everybody was real nice and we made friends.

We came to San Mateo after the war. We came out with friends. Eventually my father went to a *hakujin* family to work. Eventually, he went back to Hawaii with my mother and younger brother. I've been in San Mateo since the end of the war.

Our parents should have gotten the reparations money. A lot of our parents were gone by then. I don't think I deserve that money, per se. Not to say I didn't, but really, the parents that have passed on; they're the ones that suffered material things. For them, it's never enough.

RONALD "TUBBY" YUTAKA YOSHIDA

Current Residence: Northridge, California
Prewar Residence: San Francisco, California

T he telephone at the family business, Albert's Floral Shoppe on Fillmore Street, was ringing all day on December 7, 1941. My parents' *kyokai* (Nichiren church) and *kenjin-kai* (prefectural organization) friends had many things to talk about. They were wondering what was going on, such as who got arrested. The FBI came to our store and questioned my father [Albert Misao Yoshida]. I heard that they were rounding up many of my father's friends.

Going to school after Pearl Harbor was uneventful. I don't recall any outright racist attacks. Although it was the practice to attend Japanese School after school, I don't recall attending Japanese School (Kinmon Gakuen) after Pearl Harbor. I attended Roosevelt Junior High School. There were few Japanese American students at school. Among my classmates were Hirokazu (Clem) Nakai, Joe Kimura, Yutaka "P-Wee" Koizumi, Shoji Horikoshi, and John Juji Hada. Although we had Caucasian and Black friends at school, we mostly stuck together taking the Geary streetcar or walking to school. Sometimes we walked through the graveyard which was in back of the Municipal streetcar/bus terminal.

A number of *hakujin* came to the store wondering what we were going to do with all the store equipment and supplies. As the time for evacuation drew closer, my dad had to sell the merchandise in the store at a big loss. The most significant thing I could remember is he had to sell his prized possession—a 1938 V-8 Packard sedan—for $25.00!

Kinmon Gakuen was the assembly point to catch the bus to Tanforan Assembly Center. My mother [Tokuko Uchiwara Yoshida] was taken away by military ambulance, but they wouldn't tell us where they were taking her. Immediately after we were interned at Tanforan, my sister wrote to the Swedish Consulate telling them we did not know the whereabouts of our mother. Sweden—being a neutral country—my father thought it best to contact them for help. To avoid censorship, we sent the letter via Mr. Sam Fusco, a lawyer and a frequent visitor to Tanforan and a beloved friend of the Japanese in San Francisco.

It wasn't until about four weeks after we were in Tanforan that we were notified that my mother was interned at a hospital in San Mateo. We received a military escort to visit her for fifteen minutes. While we visited our mother, my dad was surprised to see other Japanese patients at the San Mateo hospital with relatives in Tanforan. He quickly jotted down as many names as possible so he could notify their loved ones as to their whereabouts. The government was not prepared to handle this type of crisis management.

Since my mother was bedridden, we may have received preferential treatment and were not assigned to an old horse stable in Tanforan. We were assigned to a newly built tar-papered barracks. There was another family that was with us—a mother and her daughter—who were members of our church. We were all in one room together. I think our barracks number was 97. Our neighbors were from the San Mateo area: Kitty and Dippy Yamauchi, Lil and Toshi Miyachi, and the Taguchis, to name a few.

The one thing that angers me about the evacuation was it shortened my mother's life. My mother passed away on October 22, 1942. She was one of the first to die in Topaz. She died of ovarian cancer. She had been taking radiation treatment at Stanford-Lane Hospital in San Francisco when the war started, but the trauma and disruption caused by the evacuation certainly shortened her life. She was only forty-five years old! The War Relocation Authorities (WRA) was not prepared to handle critically ill patients.

My sister, Florence, had the biggest impact on me while I was in Topaz. She became the matriarch of our family at a very young age—fifteen—when my mother was taken ill. She had to be responsible for all the domestic chores of our home. She made a lot of sacrifices, but doesn't talk about them.

Upon our arrival to Topaz, we were greeted by the remnants of the Berkeley Boy Scout Drum and Bugle Corps. It was hot and dusty environment. We were assigned to Block 4-5-C for our residence. Block 4 was relatively close to where the camp hospital was to be established and just about everyone assigned to our block were doctors, nurses, or patients who required care.

My classroom activities at Topaz are not memorable. Geometry with Miss Watanabe ("Miss Cotton Pot" as Andy Handa used to call her) was the best class. The after-school activities, like working on the school newspaper and year-book and preparing for school socials, were the highlights of my high school days. Part of my school activities were influenced by the girl I was dating, Seiko Akahoshi (Brodbeck). She was a girl with lots of personality and smarts. We went to all the school socials together and she was an especially good dancer.

I had a part-time job working at the Topaz Art School in Block 7 as a "go-fer." Whenever an artist wanted something, like supplies or cutting paper, I was the "go-to" guy. It was an interesting environment to work at. The artists at Topaz became particularly famous after camp; Obata, Hibi, Okubo, and Tsuzuki, to name a few.

I was a member of the Boy Scout Troop 12 Drum and Bugle Corps in San Francisco. During the initial year at Topaz our troop entertained at a talent show in the nearby town of Delta. I was also a member of the Jivesters, a six- or seven-piece band that played swing/jive music for talent shows and dances. I played trumpet.

I listened to the *Hit Parade*. The only jingle I can recall is "Lucky Strike Green has gone to War." They must have used green for camouflage material. The bands that I liked are Benny Goodman, Duke Ellington, Glenn Miller, and Artie Shaw. I also enjoyed listening to the Mills Brothers, Ink Spots, and the Andrews Sisters sing.

As far as fads go, I remember the girls of the Senior Girl Reserves (Daisy, Sadame, Seiko) developed a spoken language called "G" language. I'm not sure where it originated, but it was used to keep the outsiders (mainly boys) uninformed. Example: Daisy would be pronounced "Da-gay-zi-gi." Another fad was how you placed a postage stamp on an envelope to show affection for the recipient of the letter. If the postage stamp is placed upside down it meant "love." Another fad was to place initials on the postage envelope, like "I.L.T.G.T.O.T.L." which stood for "I love the girl that opens this letter." There were countless others.

Although I was underage, I applied for summer work outside of camp and went to do seasonal farm work whenever the opportunity arose. My first job was in Hurricane, Utah, in 1943 to thin sugar beets. That was a backbreaking job and they paid by piece work: the more rows you thin, the more money you make. I was lucky to barely make my room and board.

In the summer of 1944, I went to work at Pleasant Grove Cannery in Provo, Utah, to can peas. We stayed in a farm camp in Provo, Utah, and we were trucked everyday to the cannery. Many of the workers were from Topaz and Heart Mountain. I also picked pears and peaches in nearby orchards. That summer I also went to Ogden, Utah, and stayed at the Del Monte cannery barracks. There were many *Nisei* there from Minidoka. With what little money I did make during the summers, I was happy to buy clothes and records.

In the winter of '44, a group of University of California, Berkeley students came to Topaz to recruit students to enter the January '45 class. The West Coast was still a restricted area at the time. But these UC recruiters assured us that the ban on Japanese reentering the coast would soon be lifted. The recruiters were all associated with the UC student government and the YMCA and YWCA. Seiko and I applied for entry at UC and we were both accepted. We had to accelerate our senior year at Topaz in order to graduate in January instead of June. We left Topaz as a group of twelve students to begin our journey to freedom and the beginning of college life.

I have attended every class reunion of the Topaz Class of '45. The camaraderie and bond that our classmates have developed cannot be matched. I don't attend reunions of my college class or belong to any veterans group, but I do make it a point to see my high school classmates. The guiding light to all these class reunions has been Daisy Satoda, Sadame Kojimoto, and Hiko Nakaso. Without their enthusiasm and support, the class reunions would not be what it is.

From today's perspective, the Japanese American incarceration was terribly unjust. But in retrospect, I just went along with the crowd and didn't feel my civil liberties were taken away. You go with the flow...*shikata ga nai*. In the summer of 1987, my wife Miye and I took a tour of the national parks in Yellowstone, Glacier, Banff, and so on. We stopped in Salt Lake City and then went on to Delta and Topaz. We had a difficult time finding the ol' homestead, but I saw the "Topaz" plaque with its bullet-ridden holes.

AFTERWORD

Nearly sixty years have passed since members of the Topaz High School Class of 1945 graduated and were released from the confines of the Central Utah WRA Relocation Center. The preceding pages reveal that, for some, the memory of their internment has taken on the patina of simple nostalgia with the passage of time. Others perhaps more introspective in nature offer accounts rich in observed detail and deep in psychological insight. Almost all by now, however, understand the historical significance of their internment during World War II, even if certain individuals might not fully comprehend its long-term effect on their lives.

In the early planning stages of *Blossoms in the Desert*, concerns were raised whether those included in the collection would be representative of the Class of '45 in total. The goal was to present the widest possible perspective of high school life at Topaz from as many viewpoints as could be managed. Toward that end, the project organizing committee agreed that the anthology would attempt to include every Class of '45 member in the way that school yearbooks are inclusive.

Sadly, there were not a few members of the Class of '45 who over the years had distanced themselves from their friends and classmates at Topaz. When invited to contribute to *Blossoms in the Desert*, they declined to do so. Whatever personal reasons they might have in keeping their thoughts on the internment to themselves, this represents a loss both to the Japanese American community and all Americans who still have much to learn about the dark side of US history. Although *Blossoms in the Desert* succeeds in depicting the quotidian struggles and youthful promise of young men and women during a formative moment in their lives under exceptional circumstances, it is a work not quite complete in view of those who chose not to share the accumulated wisdom they possess. For those members of the Topaz High School Class of 1945 who gave generously of themselves in the making of this historic collection, present and future generations forever will be grateful.

—Darrell Y. Hamamoto, Editor

ROSTER

CLASS OF JAN '45

Akiyoshi, Sumiye
Doi, Takeko
Furuya, Yasumitsu
Handa, Andy
Hayashida, Juro
Ishihara, Shigeru
Itashiki, Elsie
Kanzaki, Keiko

Katayama, Tomoye
Kinoshita, Sachiko
Kitagaki, Kiyoshi
Kitagawa, Naomi
Kusunoki, Kiyoshi
Mabushi, Clara
Maruyama, Asako
Matsumoto, Peter

Mizuhara, ...oto
Nao, Kazu
Nomura, Shig
Ochi, Akiko
Osugi, Emily
Ozawa, Ichiro
Sakaguchi, Masaki
Sakaguchi, Toshiaki

Sasagawa, Frank
Sato, Yaeko
Shinoda, Mariko
Suyemoto, Joe
Takahashi, Mako
Takita, Aiko
Tsumori, Eimi
Yamate, Aileen
Yoshiura, Shizuye

CLASS OF JUNE, '45

Abey, Edith
Akahoshi, Seiko
Akita, Wasco
Aoyagi, Toshiko
Asazawa, Ken
Asoo, Rose
Baba, Isao
Bell, Paul
Doami, Junji
Dowke, Carvin
Egashira, June
Endow, Tomiko
Fujii, Hanako
Fujii, Violet
Fujita, James
Fukada, Mary
Fukuoka, Tommy
Furusho, Miyeko
Hada, Juji
Hamachi, Roy
Hara, Sadane
Haramaki, Yoshi
Hashimura, Sumiko
Hatashita, Nobutoshi
Hayashi, Betty
Hayashi, Yukio
Hideshima, Kazuko
Hirabayashi, Irvin
Hirose, Yetsuko
Hitomi, TeRuko
Horikoshi, Shoji
Ichisaka, Kiyoto
Ihara, Kimiye
Ikeda, Natsu
Ikeda, Ruby
Inouye, Takara
Ishibashi, Roy

Ishida, Kumiko
Ishimaru, Kenzo
Ito, Tatsuko
Iwaki, Mary
Iwasaki, Janet
Iwata, Eddie
Kajita, Yoshimi
Kariya, Kumiko
Kashiwahara, Shizuko
Kawabata, Harry
Kawamorita, Emi
Kawamoto, Shigeru
Kawamoto, Tomi
Kawamura, Roy
Kawata, Natsuko
Keikoan, Yoshiko
Kenmotsu, Sotoi
Kikuchi, Ernest
Kimura, Yoshimitsu
Keijomura, Tatsue
Kobayashi, Ayako
Kojimoto, Harumi
Kumagai, Tomiko
Kumekawa, Ryozo
Kuroko, Jane
Kuwahara, Isamu
Marubayashi, Ruri
Masuda, Tommie
Matsumoto, Mary
Matsunami, Yoshio
Mizokami, Bob
Mizota, Takeshi
Momii, Sam
Nagamoto, Masayoshi
Nagano, Florence
Nagasawa, Emiko
Nakagiri, Kikuko

Nakahira, Ritsuko
Nakai, Hirokazu
Nakamura, Betty
Nakamizo, Mitsuko
Nakamoto, Rose
Nakamura, Henry
Nakamura, Masaaki
Nakashige, Mary
Nakaso, Sam
Nakata, Akio
Namba, Shizuo
Nishikubo, George
Noda, Masaki
Nodohara, Keiso
Nomura, Dorothy
Nomura, Raymond
Nonaka, Mashahide
Ogata, Yoko
Ogawa, Midori
Ogo, Kiyoshi
Ohara, Wichi
Okada, Hiro
Okawachi, Shigekazo
Oku, Kazuye
Okumoto, Fumiko
Ono, Paul
Ota, Hiroshi
Ota, Tohru
Otsuji, Fred
Otsuki, Terumi
Saiki, Fumiko
Sakoda, Hideo
Sanjo, Richard
Sasaki, Takeo
Sato, Lena
Sato, Ruby
Sato, Teruko

Shibata, Eichi
Shimada, Ellen
Shimada, Yoshio
Shimamura, Mitsuko
Shimomura, Saburo
Shimosaka, June
Shiozawa, Peggy
Sonoda, Yuki
Sumimoto, Masaru
Suzawa, Shigeko
Takahashi, Hidetoshi
Takahashi, Mary
Takahashi, Michi
Takahashi, Toki
Takahashi, William
Takai, Akio
Takaki, Kaoru
Tamaki, Mary
Tamura, Teruyo
Tatsuguchi, Yuki
Tsuchihashi, Yuki
Tsugawa, Yumi
Tsujisaka, Alice
Uyeda, Daisy
Yamada, Amy
Yamada, Tome
Yamanaka, Henry
Yamashiro, Richard
Yoshida, Kiyoko
Yoshida, Yutaka
Yoshifuji, Yoriko
Yoshimine, Hiroko
Yoshino, Patty
Yoshiwara, Hiroko

From 1943 Ramblings Yearbook

CHRONOLOGY OF TOPAZ CLASS OF '45 REUNIONS AND MINI-REUNIONS

Date	Event	Location
Aug. 1, 1970	25th	San Francisco, Miyako Hotel
Aug. 30, 1975	30th	San Francisco, Miyako Hotel
Aug. 16, 1980	35th	San Francisco, Miyako Hotel
June, 29, 1985	40th	San Francisco, Presidio Officers' Club
Sept. 30–Oct. 2, 1987		Nisei Veterans Congressional Dinner, Washington, DC / Memorial Service at Arlington National Cemetary / '45 Get-together @ China Inn, Georgetown
Sept. 16–18, 1988		All-Topaz Reunion, Hyatt Regency, Burlingame, Calif. / '45 Mini-reunion at Benihana, Burlingame
July 21, 1990	45th	San Francisco, Presidio Officers' Club
Sept. 4–6, 1992	50th	All Topaz Reunion, Hyatt Regency, Burlingame /'45 Luncheon at Benihana, Burlingame, Calif.
Nov. 11–14, 1994		Japanese American National Museum (JANM) Family Expo, LA Convention Center—Topaz Exhibit Coordinated by Daisy Satoda
Aug. 19, 1995	50th	San Francisco, Miyako Hotel "The Last Hurrah"
Sept. 2–3, 1995		All-Topaz Reunion '95 – Los Angeles JANM America's Concentration Camp Remembers...New Otani Hotel

Date	Event	Location
Nov. 8, 1995		National Salute to JA Veterans – LA Convention Center
Aug. 3, 1996	51st	Yu-Ai-Kai Senior Center, San Jose, Calif.
Aug. 9, 1997	52nd	Mills College, Oakland, Calif.
May 29–31, 1998		All-Topaz Reunion, Doubletree Hotel, San Jose, Calif. / '45 Luncheon at Yu Ai Kai, San Jose
July, 9, 1999	54th	Sequoyah Country Club, Oakland, Calif.
Nov. 17–19, 1999		All-Topaz Mini-Reunion held in conjunction with the opening of JANM new Pavillion, visits to LACMA and Getty Museum / '45 dinner @ Akasaka Hanten
Sept. 30, 2000	55th	Sequoyah Country Club, Oakland, Calif.
Nov. 8–11, 2000		'45 Dinner @ Thai Town Restaurant / Topaz Reunion Y2K / Dedication of National Memorial to JA Patriotism, Washinton DC / '45 Luncheon @ Sam & Harry's, hosted by Dr. Ray and Mary (Tamaki) Murakami
Sept. 21–23, 2001	56th	Hosted by Tamie & Joe Kimura, Country Inn, Cardiff-by-the Sea, Calif. / Development of class anthology for proposal to California Civil Liberties Public Education Program
Aug. 31, 2002		All-Topaz Reunion 2002 Luncheon, Radisson Miyako Hotel, San Francisco / '45 Dinner at Jitalda Restaurant
Sept. 6, 2003	58th	Class of '45 Reunion at Radisson Miyako Hotel /Held in conjunction with initial book publication and signing of "Blossoms in the Desert...Topaz High School Class of '45" at the JCCCNC, San Francisco

Seiko Baba, Junji Doami, Yas
Furuya, Mary Hanamura, Kumi
Ishida, Yoshiko Keikoan, Sadame
Kojimoto, Sachi Masaoka, Clem
Nakai, Jimmy Nakamura, Hiroko
and Sam Nakaso, Daisy Satoda,
Rey Sonoda, M. Wacky Sumimoto,
Richard Yamashiro, Ronald
Yoshida.

ACKNOWLEDGEMENTS

Bank of Tokyo, Japan Center
Branch, Yas Furuya, George and
Jim's Richfield, Jack Hirose,
Honnami Taieido, Mits Kojimoto,
N. B. Department Store, Eugene
Nodohara, Richard's Jeweler,
Yone Satoda, Soko Hardware,
Sumitomo Bank of California,
Yoshida's Picture Framing.

COVER DESIGN - Original Woodblock print of Topaz by
Miye Yoshimori Yoshida

THE 25TH YEAR REUNION

OF THE CLASS OF 1945

TOPAZ HIGH SCHOOL

MIYAKO HOTEL

SAN FRANCISCO, CALIF.

AUGUST 1, 1970

PROGRAM

WELCOMING MESSAGE
                    MR. JUNJI DOAMI

INTRODUCTION OF
    MR. DAVE TATSUNO
                    MRS. SACHI MASAOKA

ADDRESS   MR. DAVE TATSUNO

FILMS OF TOPAZ

"REMEMBER THIS"
                    MRS. SEIKO BABA
        MR. M. WACKY SUMIMOTO

CLOSING REMARKS
                    MR. JUNJI DOAMI

1970 Reunion

HAIL ALMA MATER

David Iino   William Oshima

All hail Topaz High School,
A torch that our paths
    will light,
Our colors the Green and Gold,
Shall symbolize our might.
From far and wide we've
    gathered,
And made now into one,
We'll cherish this, our
    Alma Mater,
Which will not go unsung.

All hail Topaz High School,
We'll leave thee with
    spirits fine,
And hope we will prove to be
Ever worthy sons of thine.
Our steps for long you've
    guided,
And now without a fear,
We're proud to leave as
    part of you,
Our Alma Mater dear.

IN MEMORIUM

TAKESHI MIZOTA
May 28, 1927   July 12, 1956

MASAAKI SAKAGUCHI
Aug. 7, 1926   Jan. 11, 1956

LLOYD TAKEO SASAKI
Oct. 21, 1927   July 17, 1968

TOM YAMADA
1925   1952

CLASS OFFICERS

CLASS OF JANUARY 1945

ICHIRO OZAWA   President

JURO HAYASHIDA   Vice President

JUNJI DOAMI   Vice President

ASAKO MARUYAMA   Secretary

MARY TSUCHIYA   Treasurer

CLASS OF JUNE 1945

JUNJI DOAMI   President

BETTY HAYASHI   Vice President

DOROTHY HARADA   Vice President

AMY HIRONAKA   Secretary

HARRY KAWABATA   Treasurer

1970 Reunion

Hail Alma Mater

— By —

William Oshima, Lyrics — David Iino, Music

All hail, Topaz High School,
    A torch that our paths will light,

Our colors, the Green and Gold,
    Shall symbolize our might.

From far and wide we've gathered,
    And made now into one,

We'll cherish this, our Alma Mater,
    Which will not go unsung.

All hail, Topaz High School,
    We'll leave thee with spirits fine,

And hope we will prove to be
    Ever worthy sons of thine.

Our steps for long you've guided,
    And now without a fear,

We're proud to leave as part of you,
    Our Alma Mater dear.

Return to Topaz '93

Recollections

Reflections

Remembrances

Topaz Anthology

Topaz High 1945 Banner and Pennants
(designed by Ron "Tubby" Yoshida")

IN MEMORIAM

Elsie Itashiki Callegari
Sono Suzuki Fujie
Hanako Fujii
Kiyoko Yoshida Govier
Kazu Nao Harano
John "Joker" Hada
Kay Ichisaka
Chiyo Date Iino
Takara Inouye
Shig Ishihara
Edward Iwata
Shig Iyama
Chester Kaku
Harry Kawabata

Jensuke "Zane" Matsuzaki
Yosh Mihara
Takeshi Mizota
Astor Mizuhara
Joe Morita
Alan "Potay" Nakata
Shizuo Namba
Ryo Nihei
Mary Fukada Nita
Masaki Jim Noda
Naomi Kitagawa Ogawa

Kiyoshi Ogo
George Okawachi
Ichiro Ozawa
Masaaki "Machan"
   Sakaguchi
Lloyd Takeo Sasaki
Harvey Shimada
Yosh Shimada
Fumi Saiki Shiro
Takeo "Tick" Sonoda
Kimiye Ihara Spicer
Joe Suyemoto
Michio Mike Suzuki
William Takahashi
Shigeko Jacky Suzawa
   Takayanagi
Shin Tanaka
Allen Tsuchitani
Mitsue Urabe
Tom Yamada
Ichiro "Chuck" Yamasaki
Ruby Sato Yamasaki
Richard "Ratcho" Yamashiro
Takehiko Yanagi
Harry "Harbo" Yuki

(Incomplete List)

IN MEMORIAM

Elsie Itashiki Callegari

Hanako Fujii

Sono Suzuki Fujie

Kiyoko Yoshida Govier

Juji "Joker" Hada

Kazu Nao Harano

Kay Ichisaka

Chiyo Date Iino

Takara Inouye

Shig Ishihara

Edward Iwata

Chester Kaku

Harry Kawabata

Takeshi Mizota

Joe Morita

IN MEMORIAM

Alan "Potay" Nakata

Shizuo Namba

Ryo Nihei

Mary Fukada Nita

Masaki Jim Noda

Naomi Kitagawa Ogawa

Kiyoshi Ogo

George Okawachi

Ichiro Ozawa

Masaaki "Machan" Sakaguchi

Lloyd Takeo Sasaki

Harvey Shimada

Yosh Shimada

Fumi Saiki Shiro

Shigeko Suzawa Takayanagi

Kimiye Ihara Spicer

IN MEMORIAM

Joe Suyemoto

Michio Mike Suzuki

William Takahashi

Ruby Sato Yamasaki

Ichiro Chuck Yamasaki

Richard "Ratcho" Yamashiro

Takehiko Yanagi

Harry "Harbo" Yuki

Harry Kawabata & Richard Yamashiro

Chet & Shiz & Mickey

TOPAZ HIGH SCHOOL CLASS OF 1945 ROSTER

Name	Jan	June	Aug	Relo
Edith Abey		x		
Seiko Akahoshi		x		
Wasko Akita		x		
Hajime Jim Akiyama			x	
Sumiye Akiyoshi	x			
Hatsuye Aoyagi			x	
Toshiko Aoyagi		x		
Hisa Aoki				x
Ken Asazawa		x		
Rose Asoo		x		
Isao Baba		x		
Paul Bell		x		
Chiyo Date			x	
Junji Doami		x		
Takeko Doi	x			
Carvin Dowke		x		
June Egashira		x		
Tomi Endow	x			
Tak Enomoto			x	
Dewey Fujii			x	
Hanako Fujii		x		
Violet Fujii			x	
James Fujita	x			
Mary Fukada		x		
Warren Fukuhara		x		
Tommy Fukuoka				x
Miyeko Furusho		x		
Yas Furuya	x			

Name	Jan	June	Aug	Relo
Juji John Hada		x		
Roy Hamachi		x		
Takuzo Andy Handa				x
Sadame Hara		x		
Dorothy Harada			x	
Yoshi Haramaki		x		
Sumiko Hashimura				x
Nobutoshi Hatashita		x		
Betty Hayashi		x		
Yukio Hayashi				?
Juro Hayashida	x			
Kazuko Hideshima		x		
Irvin Hirabayashi				x
Amy Hironaka			x	
Mary Hironaka			x	
Lillian Hirose	x			
Terry Hitomi	x			
Shoji Horikoshi				x
Sak Horita			x	
Kay Ichisaka		x		
Kimiye Ihara		x		
Shigeru Iiyama	x			
Natsu Ikeda	x			
Ruby Ikeda		x		
Fred Ikenoyama		x		
Takara Inouye		x		
Roy Ishibashi				x
Kumi Ishida		x		
Shigeru Ishihara	x			
Kenzo Ishimaru				x
Elsie Itashiki	x			
Tatsuko Ito		x		
Mary Iwaki		x		
Sus Iwasa			x	
Janet Iwasaki		x		
Eddie Iwata		x		
Yoshimi Kajita				x
Chester Kaku			x	
Teruko Kaneko	x			
Kei Kanzaki				x
Kumiko Kariya				x
Tomi Kasai			x	

Name	Jan	June	Aug	Relo
Shizuko Kashiwabara	x			
Mary Kataoka				x
Tomoye Katayama	x			
Molly Kato				x
Dick Katayanagi				x
John Katsu				x
Harry Kawabata		x		
Tosh Kawabata			x	
Sachi Kawahara		x		
Emi Kawamorita				x
Tomi Kawamoto				x
Shigeru Kawamoto		x		
Roy Kawamura		x		
Natsuko Kawata		x		
Yoshiko Keikoan		x		
Sotoi Kenmotsu		x		
Ernest Kikuchi		x		
Joe Kimura		x		
Sachi Kinoshita	x			
Naomi Kitagawa	x			
Kiyoshi Kitagaki				x
Tatsue Kiyomura		x		
Ayako Kobayashi		X		
George Kobayashi			x	
Misao Kodani			x	
Kuni Koga				x
Harumi Kojimoto		x		
Kunio Konno			x	
Tomi Kumagai		x		
Glenn Ryozo Kumekawa		x		
Yae Kunisawa				x
Jane Kuroko				x
Kiyoshi Kusunoki				x
Isamu Kuwahara		x		
Clara Mabuchi	x			
Ruri Marubayashi		x		
Kaz Maruoka			x	
Asako Maruyama	x			
Misao Masunaga			x	
Tom Masuda		x		
Mary Matsumoto		x		
Peter Matsumoto				x
Yoshio Matsunami		x		

Name	Jan	June	Aug	Relo
Yayoe Matsushita		x		
Zane Matsuzaki				x
John Miyagawa	x			
Bob Mizokami				x
Astor Mizuhara				x
Takeshi Mizota		x		
Joe Morita			x	
Masayoshi Nagamoto		x		
Florence Nagano		x		
Emi Nagasawa		x		
Maya Nagata				x
Kiko Nakagiri		x		
Ritsuko Nakahira		x		
Clem Nakai		x		
Mits Nakamizo				x
Rose Nakamoto		x		
Betty Nakamura		x		
Henry Nakamura		x		
James Nakamura		x		
Mary Nakashige			x	
Sam Nakaso				x
Alan Akio Nakata		x		
Mits Nakata				?
Shiz Namba		x		
Kazuko Nao	x			
Ruth Naruo				x
Ryo Nihei			x	
George Nishikubo				x
Dwight Nishimura				x
James Noda		x		
Eugene Nodohara		x		
Alice Nomura				x
Dorothy Nomura	x			
Shig Nomura				x
Mas Nonaka				x
Yuri Obata				x
Ellen Akiko Ochi				x
Somao Ochi			x	
Yoko Ogata		x		
Agnes Ogawa		x		
Kiyoshi Ogo		x		
Wichi Ohara		x		
Hiro Okada		x		

Name	Jan	June	Aug	Relo
George Okawachi		x		
Kazue Oku		x		
Fumi Okumoto		x		
Paul Ono		x		
Martha Oshima			x	
Emily Osugi	x			
Hiroshi Ota		x		
Tohru Ota				x
Eiko Otagiri	x			
Fred Otsuji	x			
Terumi Otsuki		x		
Tatsuko Ozaki				x
Ichiro Ozawa	x			
Fumi Saiki		x		
Jim Sakaguchi				?
Masaaki Sakaguchi		x		
Toshiaki Sakaguchi	x			
Hideo Sakoda				
Jean Sanford		x		
Richard Sanjo		x		
Tats Sano			x	
Frank Sasagawa				x
Takeo Sasaki		x		
Lena Sato		x		
Ruby Sato		x		
Teruko Sato				x
Yaeko Sato	x			
Eichi Shibata				x
Ellen Shimada	x			
Harvey Shimada	x			
Yosh Shimada		x		
Mits Shimamura		x		
Sab Shimomura				x
June Shimosaka		x		
Mari Shinoda	x			
Peggy Shiozawa		x		
Ray Gus Sonoda			x	
Yuki Sonoda		x		
Shigeki Sugiyama				x
Chas.Wacky Sumimoto		x		
Joe Suyemoto	x			
Mike Suzuki			x	
Sono Suzuki				x
Shigeko Suzawa		x		

Name	Jan	June	Aug	Relo
Yoko Tahara				x
Leslie Takagawa			x	
Hidetoshi Takahashi		x		
Jimmy Takahashi			x	
Makoto Takahashi				x
Mary Takahashi		x		
Michi Takahashi	x			
Toki Takahashi		x		
William Takahashi		x		
Akio Takai		x		
Kaoru Takaki		x		
Kaz Takei				x
Aiko Takita	x			
Mary Tamaki	x			
Lily Tamura	x			
Teruyo Tamura		x		
Yuki Tatsuguchi				x
Yukiye Tsuchihashi		x		
Allen Tsuchitani				x
Mary Tsuchiya		x		
Yumi Tsugawa	x			
Alice Tsujisaka		x		
Eimi Tsumori				x
Bob Utsumi			x	
Daisy Uyeda		x		
Amy Yamada		x		
Tome Yamada	x			
Haruye Yamamoto				x
Henry Yamanaka		x		
Ichiro Chuck Yamasaki			x	
Richard Yamashiro		x		
Aileen Yamate	x			
Herbert Yamate		x		
Gloria Yasunaka				x
Takehiko Yanagi			x	
Takeshi Yanagi			x	
Shizuko Yokomizo				x
Kiyoko Yoshida		x		
Ron Yoshida		x		
Yae Yoshifuji		x		

Name	Jan	June	Aug	Relo
Hiroko Yoshimine				x
Patty Yoshino		x		
Kay Yoshiura			x	
Sue Yoshiura	x			
Hiroko Yoshiwara		x		
Harry Yuki		x		

NOTE: This list includes all students who were classified as Topaz High Class of 1945, which includes class members who transferred to Tule Lake in September 1943, as well as students who transferred into Topaz from Tule Lake, and also students who left camp early in order to relocate to the Mountain, Midwest and Eastern areas of the United States where they completed their high school education.

This list includes all persons who were asigned to the class of 1945: January 1945, June 1945, and August 1945. This Low Senior Class was accelerated to graduate with the June class of 1945 because the camps were closing.

ANNOTATED BIBLIOGRAPHY

Books on Topaz

Arrington, Leonard J. *The Price of Prejudice: The Japanese American Relocation Center in Utah during World War II*, 2nd ed., Delta, UT: Topaz Museum, 1997. Factual account of Topaz camp with details of internment, agriculture and employment. Updated with photographs and reprinted by the Topaz Museum.

Hill, Kimi Kodani. *Topaz Moon: Art of the Internment*. Berkeley, CA: Heyday Books, 2000. A biography of Chiura Obata who organized camp-wide art schools at Tanforan and Topaz.

Kitano, Harry H.L. *Generations and Identity: The Japanese American*. Needham Heights, MA: Ginn Press, Simon & Schuster Higher Education Publishing Group, 1993. Note: Chapter 13, page 193–194 under Diversity in Summary, Conclusions: Meeting with former Topaz High School students Amy Tamaki Doi, John Juji Hada, Sadame Hara Kojimoto, Sachi Kawahara Masaoka, Sam Nakaso, Daisy Uyeda Satoda, Asaye Ashizawa Takagi, and Aileen Yamate in San Francisco July 28, 1991.

Okubo, Mine. *Citizen 13660*. Seattle, WA: Univ. of Washington Press, 1946. Reprinted 1973, 1983. Personal account of life in Topaz with illustrations of the camp by the author.

Taylor, Sandra C. *Jewel of the Desert: Japanese American Internment at Topaz*. Berkeley, CA: Univ. of California Press, 1993. The story of San Francisco Bay Area Americans and their forced internment at Topaz, Utah, during World War II.

Tunnell, Michael O. & George W. Chilcoat. *The Children of Topaz*. New York, NY: Holiday House, 1996. Based on the diary kept by a third-grade class in Topaz.

Uchida, Yoshiko. *Desert Exile: The Uprooting of a Japanese American Family*. Seattle, WA: University of Washington Press, Third Printing,1991. The author's personal story of her family's life interrupted by the incarceration of Japanese Americans during World War II.

Books on Internment

Dempster, Brian Komei, ed. From *Our Side of the Fence: Growing up in America's Concentration Camps*. San Francisco, CA: Kearny Street Workshop, 2001. Writings of former school children, fifty-five years after their incarceration. Writers include four former residents of Topaz: Fumi Manabe Hayashi, Florence Miho Nakamura, Toru Saito, and Daisy Uyeda Satoda.

Film and Videos on Topaz

Starting Over; Japanese Americans after the War. Dianne Fukami for KCSM TV 60. 60 min./1996. Documents the struggle of Japanese Americans as they resettled throughout the US after the camps, and the prejudices they encountered as they tried to find housing and employment. Distributor: NAATA (415) 863-0814. (www.naatanet.org/distrib)

Tanforan, Race Track to Assembly Center. Dianne Fukami and Donald Young. 57 min./1995. In-depth study of the Tanforan Assembly Center in San Bruno, CA, where thousands of Japanese Americans lived before their transfer to permanent World War II concentration camps in inland USA. Distributor: NAATA (415) 863-0814. (www.naatanet.org/distrib)

Topaz. 58 minutes. Produced and directed by Ken Verdoia, Station KUED, Salt Lake City, UT, 1991. This documentary discusses the internment, contains interviews with former internees, and has footage of the camp. (www.kued.org)

Dave Tatsuno's Home Movies of Topaz, approx. 60 minutes. Video copy of movies taken with an 8mm camera smuggled into Topaz. Many scenes of everyday life in camp. Because of its outstanding cultural and historical significance, this movie footage was only the second movie added to the Library of Congress National Archives Film Registry in 1996.

Websites for Photos of Topaz

www.archive.gov
   National Archive Japanese American Internee database.
   [Click on "Research Room"]

www.topazcamp.org or www.topazmuseum.org
   Information, photographs and resources about Topaz, including brief history of the camp.

www.content.lib.utah.edu
   Find the home page of the "Marriott Library Digital Collec-
   tions." Go to "American Westward Migration", and select
   "Topaz Museum." Photos taken from scrapbook of Eleanor
   Gerard Sekerak, teacher at Topaz High School. Many of
   these photos were taken by Yas Furuya, Topaz High Class
   of January 1945.

www.oac.cdlib.org/dynaweb/ead/calher/jvac/
   Bancroft Library of University of California Berkeley. Photographs and documents relating to the internment with
   an emphasis on Bay Area Japanese American experiences.